TRUMP

V

TRUMP

SEVEN DIALS

First published in Great Britain in 2019 by Seven Dials
An imprint of Orion Publishing Group Ltd
Carmelite House, 50 Victoria Embankment, London, EC4Y

An Hachette UK Company

1 3 5 7 9 10 8 6 4 2

Text © Orion Publishing Group Ltd 2019

Illustrations from Shutterstock

A CIP catalogue record for this book is
available from the British Library.

Paperback ISBN: 9781841883977
Ebook ISBN: 9781841883960

Printed and bound in Great Britain by Clays Ltd, Elcograf, S.p.A.

MIX
Paper from
responsible sources
FSC® C104740
www.fsc.org

www.orionbooks.co.uk

CONTENTS

THE AIM OF THE GAME

The big bad media just keeps on spreading tall tales, but at long last here is a book that can help you hone your skills of fishing the truth from the lies!

Throughout this book you'll find two statements on the same subject matter. One is from the real Trump (i.e. a definitive quote from DJT about himself, other people, the rest of the world, general wisdom and happenings in the USA). The other is your average Trump (something we made up, fake news, hot air, smoke in the wind, a big fat fart). Tick the box you think is a falsehood and then flick to the end of the section to tot up how many you surmised correctly. If you . . .

. . . SCORE OVER 15: YOU'RE A TRUMP CONNOISSEUR!

You can deftly sort the Stinkers (Trumpisms) from the stinkers (fake news). You are either so disgusted with Donald Trump that you know or can correctly weed out which statement he is likely to have said, or you're a super Trump lover and understand the inner workings of his brain*.

*Be afraid, be very afraid.

. . . SCORE 10-15: YOU'RE UNSURE HOW WE GOT TO THIS POINT IN WORLD POLITICS

You're doing relatively well on figuring out the type of thing the Donald would say, but for the most part you're panicking, 'Surely he didn't really say that?!' Yes, dear reader, I'm afraid he did.

. . . SCORE UNDER 10: YOU'RE IN DENIAL

You're either optimistic about the calibre of Trump's oral skills, you need to read the papers more, or you're one of the people who voted him in.

BONUS POINTS

If you see this symbol, one of the quotes is from Trump and the other is from another world leader. Correctly identify that world leader and you can give yourself two points instead of one.

TRUMP ON TRUMP

THE QUESTIONS

1.

❑ **TRUMP:** I'm the most successful person ever to run for the presidency, by far. Nobody's ever been more successful than me. I'm the most successful person ever to run. Ross Perot isn't successful like me. Romney – I have a Gucci store that's worth more than Romney.

Or

❑ **TRUMP:** I'm the most famous person to run for the presidency and I'm not famous just because of my looks or money, it's because I made something of myself. I worked my way up. I worked hard and I won. I'm smart and people love me.

2.

❑ **TRUMP:** Maybe the rich in their castles aren't voting for me, but the working people are, the working people love me – that's what the polls say and they are right.

Or

❑ **TRUMP:** I would bet if you took a poll in the FBI I would win that poll by more than anybody's won a poll.

3.

❑ **TRUMP:** God put me on this earth to be president and save America.

Or

❑ **TRUMP:** I will be the greatest jobs president that God has ever created.

4.

❏ **TRUMP:** I think the only difference between me and the other candidates is that I'm more honest and my women are more beautiful.
Or

❏ **TRUMP:** The differences between me and the other candidates are huge, I'll get the job done. I'll tell it like it is. I'm picking off lying politicians one at a time.

5.

❏ **TRUMP:** To be blunt, people would vote for me. They just would. Why? Maybe because I'm so good looking.
Or

❏ **TRUMP:** America wants me as their president, it's a no brainer. I'm smart. I'm honest. I say it like it is, people need that.

6.

❏ **TRUMP:** I could stand in the middle of 5th Avenue and shoot somebody and I wouldn't lose voters.
Or

❏ **TRUMP:** I could streak down 5th Avenue and still wouldn't lose voters.

7.

❏ **TRUMP:** I will be so good at the military your head will spin.
Or

❏ **TRUMP:** I know all there is to know about politics. Everything. Except the military, I'll have to learn a bit more about that.

❑ **TRUMP:** The only good thing about the media (who I hate because they are so dumb) . . . is that they take some great photos of me. Photos I'm very happy to have out there. They can make me look slim and handsome, which I already am.
Or

❑ **TRUMP:** I had some beautiful pictures taken in which I had a big smile on my face. I looked happy, I looked content, I looked like a very nice person, which in theory I am.

9.

❑ **TRUMP:** Thanks – Many are saying I'm the best 140 character writer in the world. It's easy when it's fun.
Or

❑ **TRUMP:** I could tweet in my sleep and still have 40 million followers.

10.

❑ **TRUMP:** Marco Rubio referred to my hands, if they are small, something else must be small. I guarantee you there is no problem. I guarantee.
Or

❑ **TRUMP:** You know what they say about big hands. And trust me, I have really, really big hands. Hands that I use very well too.

11.

❑ **TRUMP:** My hair defines me. It's what people associate with me. My definition is success and wealth and having lots of money. So I'm keeping the hair.
Or

❑ **TRUMP:** I will never change this hairstyle, I like it. It fits my head. Those who criticize me are only losers and envy people. And it is not a wig, it's my hair. Do you want to touch it?

12.

- ❑ **TRUMP:** When I look at myself in the first grade and I look at myself now, I'm basically the same. The temperament is not that different.
  Or
- ❑ **TRUMP:** I've grown and learnt so much over the last few years. I've really changed. Not that I needed to, I could have stayed the same and still done a great job, but I have changed.

13.

- ❑ **TRUMP:** If you asked me what my favourite part of my body would be, I would say my feet. You haven't seen them. Not many people have seen them properly, but they are really nice feet.
  Or
- ❑ **TRUMP:** My fingers are long and beautiful, as, it has been well documented, are various other parts of my body.

14.

- ❑ **TRUMP:** Donald Trump is a super smart guy. The smartest.
  Or
- ❑ **TRUMP:** Nobody has better respect for intelligence than Donald Trump.

15.

- ❑ **TRUMP:** No animals have been harmed in the creation of my hairstyle.
  Or
- ❑ **TRUMP:** I am not wearing a wig, but if I was it would be none of your business.

❏ **TRUMP:** I look very much forward to showing my financials, because they are huge.
Or

❏ **TRUMP:** My property portfolio is huge. And I mean huge. Really huge.

17.

❏ **TRUMP:** I came from nothing and I worked hard. I'm the true American dream success story.
Or

❏ **TRUMP:** I think that would qualify as not smart, but genius . . . and a very stable genius at that!

18.

❏ **TRUMP:** As Everybody knows, but the haters and losers refuse to acknowledge, I do not wear a 'wig'. My hair may not be perfect but it's mine.
Or

❏ **TRUMP:** I only wear a wig sometimes when I need to. And why not? Everyone else does it! I bet you more people are wearing wigs than you think.

19.

❏ **TRUMP:** When dummies think they are offending me, they need to remember that I know I'm better than them, so why would I care?
Or

❏ **TRUMP:** It makes me feel so good to hit 'sleazebags' back – much better than seeing a psychiatrist (which I never have!)

20.

☐ **TRUMP:** Isn't it crazy, I'm worth billions of dollars, employ thousands of people, and get labeled by moron bloggers who can't afford a suit! WILD.

Or

☐ **TRUMP:** Twitter is WEIRD. I can say one thing and people get so OFFENDED and all the keyboard warriors come out and say stupid things that don't make sense. That's not a comeback!

21.

☐ **TRUMP:** How come every time I show anger, disgust or impatience, enemies say I had a tantrum or meltdown – stupid or dishonest people?

Or

☐ **TRUMP:** I have never had a tantrum in my life, even when I was four, even when I was two. Emotions get in the way if you let them and enemies better learn that fast.

22.

☐ **TRUMP:** Of course, if necessary, I could be married in twenty-four hours . . . It would be very easy. Believe me.

Or

☐ **TRUMP:** Marriage is a sacred thing. It doesn't always work out, but it should be thought through. Lots of people would like to be married to me. Melania is lucky.

❑ **TRUMP:** Sorry losers and haters, but my IQ is one of the highest – and you all know it! Please don't feel so stupid or insecure, it's not your fault.

Or

❑ **TRUMP:** I was by far the smartest, the top in my class at Pennsylvania, those saying otherwise are haters and I can prove it – who else do you know from Wharton who made it the way I did? Nobody can say they've done TV and made the millions I have.

24.

❑ **TRUMP:** They asked me to be a frontman for Viagra in the 90s, I don't know why. I helped them out, really, I told them – no one will believe I take it. I said use Michael Bloomberg instead.

Or

❑ **TRUMP:** I think Viagra is wonderful if you need it, if you have medical issues, if you've had surgery. I've just never needed it. Frankly, I wouldn't mind there were an anti-Viagra, something with the opposite effect.

25.

❑ **TRUMP:** They loved me on Home Alone 2. I'm the most memorable thing about that film. Sorry Macaulay!

Or

❑ **TRUMP:** All of the women on The Apprentice flirted with me – consciously or unconsciously. That's to be expected.

26.

❑ **TRUMP:** I'm intelligent. Some people would say I'm very, very, very intelligent.

Or

❑ **TRUMP:** My mind works in amazing ways, it surprises me sometimes how smart I am.

☐ **TRUMP:** I know words, I have the best words.
Or

☐ **TRUMP:** I was too good for my Ivy League school, too smart for them.

28.

☐ **TRUMP:** Part of the beauty of me is that I am very rich.
Or

☐ **TRUMP:** I'm definitely much more happy now that I am one of the mega-rich.

29.

☐ **TRUMP:** I've had to turn down a lot of covers. At the end of the day, its not my job. I'm not a supermodel. I'm a business man.
Or

☐ **TRUMP:** You know, look, I'm on a lot of covers. I think maybe more than almost any supermodel. I think more than any supermodel.

30.

☐ **TRUMP:** I only eat the dough on pizzas, buy a margarita and scrape off the cheese.
Or

☐ **TRUMP:** I scrape the toppings off my pizza – I never eat the dough.

31.

☐ **TRUMP:** I never fall for scams. I am the only person who immediately walked out of my 'Ali G' interview.
Or

☐ **TRUMP:** Trust me, I've been interviewed by stupider people than Ali G!

32.

❑ **TRUMP:** My twitter changes people's lives. People have told me that. They told me that they read something and it changed their lives.

Or

❑ **TRUMP:** My twitter has become so powerful that I can actually make my enemies tell the truth.

33.

❑ **TRUMP:** I'm actually a nice person. I try very hard to be a nice person.

Or

❑ **TRUMP:** I don't care about being a nice person. I care about making America great again.

34.

❑ **TRUMP:** I would want George Clooney [to play me in a movie]. He's an older guy, he's great looking, he's charming, he's funny. And now he's married to a very beautiful woman.

Or

❑ **TRUMP:** Someone really really handsome [should play me in a movie]. That's the only thing that matters. I don't care if he can act well. He's got to be really, really good looking, OK?

35.

❑ **TRUMP:** I enjoy testing friendships.

Or

❑ **TRUMP:** Making enemies is more fun than making friends.

❏ **TRUMP:** People say my taste is tacky. I'm not tacky. I have enough money to buy anything. And I choose to buy the best. Since when was a huge chandelier tacky?

Or

❏ **TRUMP:** People say the '80s are dead, all the luxury, the extravagance. I say, what? Am I supposed to change my taste because it's a new decade? That's bullshit.

37.

❏ **TRUMP:** Oftentimes when I was sleeping with one of the top women in the world, I would say to myself, thinking about me as a boy from Queens, can you believe what I am getting?

Or

❏ **TRUMP:** I was always destined for great things. If you had asked me, when I was a boy living in Queens, where I want to be in the future, I would have said rich and sleeping with amazing women and both are true.

38.

❏ **TRUMP:** I would never buy Ivanka any decent jewels or pictures. Why give her negotiable assets?

Or

❏ **TRUMP:** I buy Ivanka anything she wants. She can have absolutely anything. She's a daddy's girl.

39.

❏ **TRUMP:** I am all alone (poor me) in the White House.

Or

❏ **TRUMP:** I can't believe I live in the White House now.

40.

☐ **TRUMP:** It's OK to be wrong. Being wrong leads to learning and learning leads to winning.
Or

☐ **TRUMP:** I think I'm right. And when I think I'm right, nothing bothers me.

41.

☐ **TRUMP:** I am the least racist person there is.
Or

☐ **TRUMP:** People are too sensitive, that wasn't racist.

42.

☐ **TRUMP:** And did you know my name is in more black songs than any other name in hip-hop?
Or

☐ **TRUMP:** I've had more cameos than any other celebrity. I'm basically an actor.

43.

☐ **TRUMP:** I have the world's greatest memory.
Or

☐ **TRUMP:** I know what everyone is thinking. It's like a superpower.

44.

☐ **TRUMP:** I would never sleep with a married woman. Unless they were beautiful.
Or

☐ **TRUMP:** I did try and f--- her. She was married.

45.

☐ **TRUMP:** You know I'm automatically attracted to beautiful – I just start kissing them. It's like a magnet. Just kiss. I don't even wait.

Or

☐ **TRUMP:** You don't need to ask them [women] for permission. I'm me, I can make the assumption that they want me.

46.

☐ **TRUMP:** Who knows what's in the deepest part of my mind?

Or

☐ **TRUMP:** My mind works in weird and wonderful ways, it's so full of knowledge.

47.

☐ **TRUMP:** I'm an expert in PR. Managing media and communications is totally my thing. It's easy, I've been doing it for so many years.

Or

☐ **TRUMP:** I am a handwriting analyst. Jack Lew's handwriting shows, while strange, that he is very secretive – not necessarily a bad thing.

48.

☐ **TRUMP:** I am a young, vibrant man.

Or

☐ **TRUMP:** I'm too old for this.

49.

☐ **TRUMP:** I don't call it thin-skinned. I'm angry.

Or

☐ **TRUMP:** I'm very thick- skinned, say anything. I. Do. Not. Care.

❑ **TRUMP:** I buy a slightly smaller than large glove.
   Or
❑ **TRUMP:** Its hard for me to find gloves large enough for my
   hands.

THE ANSWERS

1.

 TRUMP: I'm the most successful person ever to run for the presidency, by far. Nobody's ever been more successful than me. I'm the most successful person ever to run. Ross Perot isn't successful like me. Romney – I have a Gucci store that's worth more than Romney.[1]

Or

FAKE **TRUMP:** I'm the most famous person to run for the presidency and I'm not famous just because of my looks or money, it's because I made something of myself. I worked my way up. I worked hard and I won. I'm smart and people love me.

Trump hasn't really defined successful here. But we all know he's not afraid to big himself up!

2.

FAKE **TRUE:** Maybe the rich in their castles aren't voting for me, but the working people are, the working people love me – that's what the polls say and they are right.

Or

 TRUE: I would bet if you took a poll in the FBI I would win that poll by more than anybody's won a poll.[2]

Not according to former FBI director James Comey,[3] who urged people to vote Democrat.

---

1   *The Des Moines Register*, 2 June 2015
2   *Fox & Friends*, 15 June 2018
3   Twitter, 18 July 2018

3.

 FAKE **TRUMP:** God put me on this earth to be president and save America.

Or

 TRUMP: I will be the greatest jobs president that God has ever created.[4]

Not a bad thing to aim for, to be fair.

4.

 TRUMP: I think the only difference between me and the other candidates is that I'm more honest and my women are more beautiful.[5]

Or

FAKE **TRUMP:** The differences between me and the other candidates are huge, I'll get the job done. I'll tell it like it is. I'm picking off lying politicians one at a time.

And honesty IS the best policy. Except when your honesty objectifies women, then it's better to be quiet and stop it.

5.

 TRUMP: To be blunt, people would vote for me. They just would. Why? Maybe because I'm so good looking.[6]

Or

 FAKE **TRUMP:** America wants me as their president, it's a no brainer. I'm smart. I'm honest. I say it like it is, people need that.

Donald being modest again. I wonder how many of the 62,984,825[7] people voted for him because of his face.

---

4   Speech at Trump Tower, 16 June 2015
5   *New York Times*, November 1999
6   *New York Times*, 19 September 1999
7   https://edition.cnn.com/election/2016/results/president

6.

TRUMP: I could stand in the middle of 5th Avenue and shoot somebody and I wouldn't lose voters.[8]

Or

FAKE **TRUMP:** I could streak down 5th Avenue and still wouldn't lose voters.

Let's hope this isn't true (either of them).

7.

TRUMP: I will be so good at the military your head will spin.[9]

Or

FAKE **TRUMP:** I know all there is to know about politics. Everything. Except the military, I'll have to learn a bit more about that.

8.

FAKE **TRUMP:** The only good thing about the media (who I hate because they are so dumb) . . . is that they take some great photos of me. Photos I'm very happy to have out there. They can make me look slim and handsome, which I already am.

Or

TRUMP: I had some beautiful pictures taken in which I had a big smile on my face. I looked happy, I looked content, I looked like a very nice person, which in theory I am.[10]

In theory . . .

---

8   Campaign rally, Iowa, 23 January 2016
9   *The Hugh Hewitt Show*, 2015
10 *Crippled America: How to Make America Great Again*, 2015

9.

 TRUMP: Thanks- Many are saying I'm the best 140 character writer in the world. It's easy when it's fun.[11]

Or

 TRUMP: I could tweet in my sleep and still have 40 million followers.

To be fair, at the time of writing (May 2019) he does have 60.2 million followers[12] on Twitter. Not as many as Taylor Swift though (83.3 million).[13]

10.

 TRUMP: Marco Rubio referred to my hands, if they are small, something else must be small. I guarantee you there is no problem. I guarantee.[14]

Or

 TRUMP: You know what they say about big hands. And trust me, I have really, really big hands. Hands that I use very well too.

Information we did not need there.

---

11   Twitter, 10 November 2012
12   https://twitter.com/realDonaldTrump?lang=en
13   https://twitter.com/taylorswift13
14   *Washington Post*, 2016

11.

 TRUMP: My hair defines me. It's what people associate with me. My definition is success and wealth and having lots of money. So I'm keeping the hair.

Or

 TRUMP: I will never change this hairstyle, I like it. It fits my head. Those who criticize me are only losers and envy people. And it is not a wig, it's my hair. Do you want to touch it?[15]

I don't want to touch it. But we're pleased Trump is embracing what he was born with!

12.

 TRUMP: When I look at myself in the first grade and I look at myself now, I'm basically the same. The temperament is not that different.[16]

Or

 TRUMP: I've grown and learnt so much over the last few years. I've really changed. Not that I needed to, I could have stayed the same and still done a great job, but I have changed.

Trump admitting that he acts like a six-year-old – solid gold!

---

15   *Forbes*, 2014
16   *Never Enough: Donald Trump and the Pursuit of Success*, 2015

13.

 TRUMP: If you asked me what my favourite part of my body would be, I would say my feet. You haven't seen them. Not many people have seen them properly, but they are really nice feet.

Or

 TRUMP: My fingers are long and beautiful, as, it has been well documented, are various other parts of my body.[17]

Again, giving us information that we do not need or ever want to hear again.

14.

 TRUMP: Donald Trump is a super smart guy. The smartest.

Or

 TRUMP: Nobody has better respect for intelligence than Donald Trump.[18]

Why is he speaking about himself in the third person?

15.

 TRUMP: No animals have been harmed in the creation of my hairstyle.[19]

Or

 TRUMP: I am not wearing a wig, but if I was it would be none of your business.

This is actually pretty funny for Donald.

---

17 *New York Post*, 2011
18 CNN, 11 August 2017
19 *Trump: How to Get Rich*, 2004

16.

 TRUMP: I look very much forward to showing my financials, because they are huge.[20]

Or

 TRUMP: My property portfolio is huge. And I mean huge. Really huge.

Can we stop giving him opportunities to talk about them?

17.

TRUMP: I came from nothing and I worked hard. I'm the true American dream success story.

Or

 TRUMP: I think that would qualify as not smart, but genius . . . and a very stable genius at that![21]

Democrats introduced the 'Stable Genius Act' which dictates that presidential candidates should take a mental health test. The name of this act would have been in reference to this tweet.[22]

---

20   *TIME*, 4 April 2011
21   Twitter, 6 January 2018
22   https://www.independent.co.uk/news/world/americas/us-politics/ stable-genius-act-trump-mental-health-democrats-bill-a8150491.html

TRUMP: As Everybody knows, but the haters and losers refuse to acknowledge, I do not wear a 'wig'. My hair may not be perfect but it's mine.[23]

Or

 TRUMP: I only wear a wig sometimes when I need to. And why not? Everyone else does it! I bet you more people are wearing wigs than you think.

Trump has spoken a lot about his hair, defending claims that it is not a wig. This is probably the first time we've heard him being slightly self-deprecating though.

19.

 TRUMP: When dummies think they are offending me, they need to remember that I know I'm better than them, so why would I care?

Or

 TRUMP: It makes me feel so good to hit 'sleazebags' back – much better than seeing a psychiatrist (which I never have!)[24]

There's nothing wrong with seeing a psychiatrist, Donald.

---

23 Twitter, 24 April 2014
24 Twitter, 19 November 2012

TRUMP: Isn't it crazy, I'm worth billions of dollars, employ thousands of people, and get libeled by moron bloggers who can't afford a suit! WILD.[25]

Or

TRUMP: Twitter is WEIRD. I can say one thing and people get so OFFENDED and all the keyboard warriors come out and say stupid things that don't make sense. That's not a comeback!

Never misses the opportunity to talk about how much he is worth.

21.

TRUMP: How come every time I show anger, disgust or impatience, enemies say I had a tantrum or meltdown—stupid or dishonest people?[26]

Or

TRUMP: I have never had a tantrum in my life, even when I was four, even when I was two. Emotions get in the way if you let them and enemies better learn that fast.

Just leave him alone already!

---

25 Twitter, 19 February 2014
26 Twitter, 12 November 2012

22.

 TRUMP: Of course, if necessary, I could be married in twenty-four hours . . . It would be very easy. Believe me.[27]
Or

 TRUMP: Marriage is a sacred thing. It doesn't always work out, but it should be thought through. Lots of people would like to be married to me. Melania is lucky.

When would this be necessary?

23.

 TRUMP: Sorry losers and haters, but my IQ is one of the highest – and you all know it! Please don't feel so stupid or insecure, it's not your fault.[28]
Or

 TRUMP: I was by far the smartest, the top in my class at Pennsylvania, those saying otherwise are haters and I can prove it – who else do you know from Wharton who made it the way I did? Nobody can say they've done TV and made the millions I have.

Trump being particularly modest here.

27 *New York Times*, 19 September 1999
28 Twitter, 9 May 2013

24.

 TRUMP: They asked me to be a frontman for Viagra in the 90s, I don't know why. I helped them out, really, I told them – no one will believe I take it. I said use Michael Bloomberg instead.
Or

 TRUMP: I think Viagra is wonderful if you need it, if you have medical issues, if you've had surgery. I've just never needed it. Frankly, I wouldn't mind there were an anti-Viagra, something with the opposite effect.[29]

Trump <3 Viagra, not that he uses it.

25.

 TRUMP: They loved me on Home Alone 2. I'm the most memorable thing about that film. Sorry Macaulay!
Or

 TRUMP: All of the women on The Apprentice flirted with me – consciously or unconsciously. That's to be expected.[30]

The confidence amazes me.

26.

 TRUMP: I'm intelligent. Some people would say I'm very, very, very intelligent.[31]
Or

 TRUMP: My mind works in amazing ways, it surprises me sometimes how smart I am.

It's so nice he has such a complimentary support network.

---

29 *Playboy*, October 2014
30 *Trump: How To Get Rich*, 2004
31 *Fortune*, 3 April 2000

27.

 TRUMP: I know words, I have the best words.[32]
Or

 FAKE **TRUMP:** I was too good for my Ivy League school, too smart for them.

Words are his thing.

28.

 TRUMP: Part of the beauty of me is that I am very rich.[33]
Or

 FAKE **TRUMP:** I'm definitely much more happy now that I am one of the mega-rich.

He doesn't like to mention it, but he has quite a lot of money.

29.

 FAKE **TRUMP:** I've had to turn down a lot of covers. At the end of the day, it's not my job. I'm not a supermodel. I'm a business man.
Or

 TRUMP: You know, look, I'm on a lot of covers. I think maybe more than almost any supermodel. I think more than any supermodel.[34]

Think being the operative word here.

---

32 Campaign rally, Hilton Head, 30 December 2015
33 *Good Morning America*, 3 July 2011
34 *60 Minutes*, 27 September 2015

30.

 FAKE **TRUMP:** I only eat the dough on pizzas, buy a margarita and scrape off the cheese.

Or

 TRUMP: I scrape the toppings off my pizza – I never eat the dough.[35]

Each to their own.

31.

 TRUMP: I never fall for scams. I am the only person who immediately walked out of my 'Ali G' interview.[36]

Or

 FAKE **TRUMP:** Trust me, I've been interviewed by stupider people than Ali G!

Immediately? Ali G definitely got through a few questions!

32.

 FAKE **TRUMP:** My twitter changes people's lives. People have told me that. They told me that they read something and it changed their lives.

Or

 TRUMP: My twitter has become so powerful that I can actually make my enemies tell the truth.[37]

Who now?

---

35   *Us Weekly*, 17 September 2015
36   Twitter, 30 September 2012
37   Twitter, 17 September 2012

33.

TRUMP: I'm actually a nice person. I try very hard to be a nice person.[38]

Or

FAKE **TRUMP:** I don't care about being a nice person. I care about making America great again.

When you have to say 'actually'...

34.

FAKE **TRUMP:** I would want George Clooney [to play me in a movie]. He's an older guy, he's great looking, he's charming, he's funny. And now he's married to a very beautiful woman.

Or

TRUMP: Someone really really handsome [should play me in a movie]. That's the only thing that matters. I don't care if he can act well. He's got to be really, really good looking, OK?[39]

OK, Zoolander.

35.

TRUMP: I enjoy testing friendships.[40]

Or

FAKE **TRUMP:** Making enemies is more fun than making friends.

One more reason we're glad we're not friends.

38 *Fox News*, 28 September 2014
39 *Hollywood Reporter*, August 2015
40 *Playboy*, March 1990

36.

FAKE **TRUMP:** People say my taste is tacky. I'm not tacky. I have enough money to buy anything. And I choose to buy the best. Since when was a huge chandelier tacky?

Or

TRUMP: People say the '80s are dead, all the luxury, the extravagance. I say, what? Am I supposed to change my taste because it's a new decade? That's bullshit.[41]

Bring back animal print wallpaper, we say.

37.

TRUMP: Oftentimes when I was sleeping with one of the top women in the world, I would say to myself, thinking about me as a boy from Queens, 'can you believe what I am getting?'[42]

Or

FAKE **TRUMP:** I was always destined for great things. If you had asked me, when I was a boy living in Queens, where I want to be in the future, I would have said rich and sleeping with amazing women and both are true.

What's DJT's criteria for 'top women' do you think? Wait, not sure we want to know.

---

41 *Playboy*, March 1997
42 *Think Big: Make It Happen in Business and Life*, 2008

38.

TRUMP: I would never buy Ivanka any decent jewels or pictures. Why give her negotiable assets?[43]

Or

 TRUMP: I buy Ivanka anything she wants. She can have absolutely anything. She's a daddy's girl.

Father of the year.

39.

TRUMP: I am all alone (poor me) in the White House.[44]

Or

 TRUMP: I can't believe I live in the White House now.

All alone, twiddling his thumbs.

40.

 TRUMP: It's OK to be wrong. Being wrong leads to learning and learning leads to winning

Or

TRUMP: I think I'm right. And when I think I'm right, nothing bothers me.[45]

It must be nice to be right all the time.

41.

TRUMP: I am the least racist person there is.[46]

Or

TRUMP: People are too sensitive, that wasn't racist.

When you have to say it . . .

---

43 *Vanity Fair*, September 1990
44 Twitter, 24 December 2018
45 *60 Minutes*, 1985
46 *Fox & Friends, Fox News*, 9 May 2011

42.

TRUMP: And did you know my name is in more black songs than any other name in hip-hop?[47]

Or

TRUMP: I've had more cameos than any other celebrity, I'm basically an actor.

He does actually pop up quite a bit. Just not always in good ways.

43.

TRUMP: I have the world's greatest memory.[48]

Or

TRUMP: I know what everyone is thinking. It's like a superpower.

We don't believe this is true.

44.

TRUMP: I would never sleep with a married woman. Unless they were beautiful.

Or

TRUMP: I did try and f--- her. She was married.[49]

This is one of the many pretty terrible things Trump said in the infamous Access Hollywood *tape, which came out during Trump's election campaign.*

---

47   *Playboy*, October 2004
48   Speaking on *NBC News*, 24 November 2015
49   *Access Hollywood* tape, 2005

45.

 TRUMP: You know I'm automatically attracted to beautiful — I just start kissing them. It's like a magnet. Just kiss. I don't even wait.[50]

Or

 FAKE TRUMP: You don't need to ask them [women] for permission. I'm me, I can make the assumption that they want me.

Another terrible quote from the Access Hollywood *tape.*

46.

 TRUMP: Who knows what's in the deepest part of my mind?[51]

Or

 FAKE TRUMP: My mind works in weird and wonderful ways, it's so full of knowledge.

Do we want to know??

47.

 FAKE TRUMP: I'm an expert in PR. Managing media and communications is totally my thing. It's easy, I've been doing it for so many years.

Or

 TRUMP: I am a handwriting analyst. Jack Lew's handwriting shows, while strange, that he is very secretive – not necessarily a bad thing.[52]

Wait, Donald Trump is a handwriting analyst?

---

50   *Access Hollywood* tape, 2005
51   *BuzzFeed*, 14 February 2014
52   Twitter, 14 January 2013

48.

 TRUMP: I am a young, vibrant man.[53]

Or

 TRUMP: I'm too old for this.

Trump was the oldest person ever to become US president when he took office in January 2017 at the age of 70 years and 220 days, but Biden and Sanders would surpass his record.[54]

49.

 TRUMP: I don't call it thin-skinned. I'm angry.[55]

Or

FAKE **TRUMP:** I'm very thick-skinned, say anything. I. Do. Not. Care

Okeydoke.

50.

 TRUMP: I buy a slightly smaller than large glove.[56]

Or

 FAKE **TRUMP:** It's hard for me to find gloves large enough for my hands.

You buy a small glove then?

53 White House speech, 26 April 2019
54 https://thehill.com/homenews/administration/440803-trump-i-am-a-young-vibrant-man
55 *60 Minutes*, September 2015
56 CNN, 21 March 2016

PEOPLE

THE QUESTIONS

1.

☐ **TRUMP:** If Obama resigns from office NOW, thereby doing a great service to the country – I will give him free lifetime golf at any of my courses!

Or

☐ **TRUMP:** If Hillary wins, she can stay in Trump Tower for free for the rest of her life. That's a promise. That's how much I know she won't win.

2.

☐ **TRUMP:** Obama trying to woo us all by singing foolishly at a formal event – what a travesty!

Or

☐ **TRUMP:** Why is Obama playing basketball today? That is why our country is in trouble!

3.

☐ **TRUMP:** If Hillary Clinton can't satisfy her husband what makes her think she can satisfy America?

Or

☐ **TRUMP:** Hillary's the least qualified person I know who could be president, @AlecBaldwin would do a better job and that's saying something.

❏ **TRUMP:** Germany's, like, sitting back silent collecting money and making a fortune with probably the greatest leader in the world today, Merkel.

Or

❏ **TRUMP:** Merkel is a leader I can't have a proper conversation with because she doesn't understand what it is to need a wall.

5.

❏ **TRUMP:** If Ivanka weren't my daughter, perhaps I'd be dating her. Is that terrible?

Or

❏ **TRUMP:** Ivanka is the cleverest of my children, just the cleverest. Eric tries but what you gonna do.

6.

❏ **TRUMP:** Sad face for @katyperry, you have a big heart and Russell Brand looked good next to you.

Or

❏ **TRUMP:** @katyperry Katy, what the hell were you thinking when you married loser Russell Brand. There is a guy who has got nothing going, a waste!

7.

❏ **TRUMP:** Meryl Streep, one of the most over-rated actresses in Hollywood, doesn't know me but attacked last night at the Golden Globes. She is a . . .

Or

❏ **TRUMP:** Meryl Streep tried to offend me last night at the Golden Globes. I was more offended by her 'acting' in Into the Woods.

8.

☐ **TRUMP:** Obama is, without question the WORST EVER president. I predict he will now do something really bad and totally stupid to show manhood!
Or

☐ **TRUMP:** Everyone saying we were too late to help New Orleans after Katrina – I actually think Bush has done a great job.

9.

☐ **TRUMP:** Why would Kim Jong-un insult me by calling me 'old,' when I would NEVER call him 'short and fat?' Oh well, I try so hard to be his friend - and maybe someday that will happen!
Or

☐ **TRUMP:** Putin is a strong leader, we could learn a lot from him. We are not *best* friends, but I'd like to be his friend. A friendship where I would always get what I want.

10.

☐ **TRUMP:** My son is handsome, so handsome. He gets his looks from his father. I hope he looks this good when he is my age.
Or

☐ **TRUMP:** Every guy in the country wants to go out with my daughter.

11.

☐ **TRUMP:** How amazing, the State Health Director who verified copies of Obama's "birth certificate" died in plane crash today. All others lived.
Or

☐ **TRUMP:** People won't want a president that's not American born and bred – it's actually, you know, illegal to have one. That's why I called Obama's into question, it's called clever politic tactics.

12.

❑ **TRUMP:** Everyone knows I am right that Robert Pattinson should dump Kristen Stewart. In a couple of years, he will thank me. Be smart, Robert.

Or

❑ **TRUMP:** Robert Pattinson and Kristen Stewart make a fantastic couple. In Twilight and outside of Twilight. I'm a fan of the Twilight franchise, a big fan.

13.

❑ **TRUMP:** Kim Kardashian is the hottest one. She's not my type, but she is definitely the hottest one.

Or

❑ **TRUMP:** In the old days, they'd say she's [Kim Kardashian] got a bad body.

14.

❑ **TRUMP:** I have nothing to say about her [Cher]. Sonny was the talented one. I think she knows that.

Or

❑ **TRUMP:** Cher is somewhat of a loser. She's lonely. She's unhappy. She's very miserable.

15.

❑ **TRUMP:** @arianahuff is unattractive both inside and out. I fully understand why her former husband left her for a man – he made a good decision

Or

❑ **TRUMP:** @Jeffreyzucker, president of CNN is a mess. His looks are terrible, I mean terrible. I don't want to sound like a mean person, but his looks are really terrible.

16.

☐ **TRUMP:** Barney Frank looked disgusting – nipples protruding – in his blue shirt before congress. Very very disrespectful.
Or

☐ **TRUMP:** Barney Frank's too-tight trousers were embarrassing. I don't want to see THAT thank you very much. He is a professional . . . so rude.

17.

☐ **TRUMP:** #JebBush has to like Mexican illegals because of his wife.
Or

☐ **TRUMP:** Who's worse than George Bush? #JebBush. What an idiot

18.

☐ **TRUMP:** The concept of . . . [Hillary Clinton's] listening tour is ridiculous. People want ideas. Do you think Winston Churchill, when he was stopping Hitler, went around listening?
Or

☐ **TRUMP:** Hillary Clinton has so many secrets now she's finding them hard to juggle. She's not smart enough to juggle them. I don't want to sound controversial, but Hitler had a lot of secrets.

19.

☐ **TRUMP:** My life is full of phone calls. Too many phone calls. Me having to say no to everyone. I'm so in demand. They all want me but I'm too busy – sorry Jay Leno.
Or

☐ **TRUMP:** Jay Leno and his people are constantly calling me to go on his show. My answer is always no because his show sucks. They love my ratings!

❑ **TRUMP:** I didn't want to say anything because the haters and losers will tell me I'm being politically incorrect. But I don't care – @LadyGaga, it's a no from me.

Or

❑ **TRUMP:** While @BetteMidler is an extremely unattractive woman, I refuse to say that because I always insist on being politically correct.

21.

❑ **TRUMP:** I hate both of them [*The Apprentice* and Alan Sugar]. I can't bear Alan Sugar [he was reported to have said].

Or

❑ **TRUMP:** Dopey @Lord_Sugar I'm worth $8 billion and you're worth peanuts . . . without my show nobody would even know who you are.

❑ **WORLD LEADER:** . . . .

22.

❑ **TRUMP:** @BarackObama hard at work yesterday shooting a marshmallow cannon in the WH East Room while our country burns.

Or

❑ **TRUMP:** @HillaryClinton has spent most of her campaign tour shopping rather than working like me – we can't have a president who only shops!

23.

❑ **TRUMP:** Hillary's downfall was lying. America does not deserve to be lied to . . . I've never lied in my life. Not once. Not once have I lied and that's the truth. Hillary is lying every day and you can tell. She doesn't look comfortable, she doesn't look stable. I'm the most stable person in the world.

Or

❑ **TRUMP:** Actually, throughout my life, my two greatest assets have been mental stability and being, like, really smart. Crooked Hillary Clinton also played these cards very hard and, as everyone knows, went down in flames. I went from VERY successful businessman, to top T.V. Star.

24.

❑ **TRUMP:** @AlexSalmond of Scotland may be the dumbest leader of the free world. I can't imagine that anyone wants him in office.

Or

❑ **TRUMP:** Stupid @AlexSalmond sitting there in Scotland not having a clue what he is doing. Someone give the guy some tips!

25.

❑ **TRUMP:** No no no. I refuse to watch Family Guy. Stupid TV show with stupid characters. Written by a bunch of people with no brains and a gross sense of humour.

Or

❑ **TRUMP:** Just tried watching Modern Family – written by a moron, really boring. Writer has the mind of a very dumb and backward child. Sorry Danny!

26.

☐ **TRUMP:** Why does @BarackObama always have to rely on teleprompters?

Or

☐ **TRUMP:** Bad performance by Crooked Hillary Clinton! Reading poorly from the teleprompter! She doesn't even look presidential!

27.

☐ **TRUMP:** @cher – I don't wear a 'rug' – it's mine. And I promise not to talk about your massive plastic surgeries that didn't work.

Or

☐ **TRUMP:** I don't give a s*** what @cardib says about my hair. It looks better than her wig. At least mine is ALL MINE.

28.

☐ **TRUMP:** Great personality and very smart [Kim Jong-un]. Good combination . . . learned he's a very talented man. I also learned that he loves his country very much.

Or

☐ **TRUMP:** Kim Jong-un of North Korea is crazy. He's just crazy. He needs better security.

29.

☐ **TRUMP:** The media is a parasite. Spreading FAKE NEWS wherever they go. Don't believe a word of it, not one word. The greatest thing that I have ever done is have THIS REALISATION.

Or

☐ **TRUMP:** The media is really the word – I think one of the greatest of all terms I've come up with is fake. I guess other people have used it perhaps over the years, but I've never noticed it.

30.

☐ **TRUMP:** The man [Bill Clinton] couldn't even be loyal to his wife. I've had many offers, trust me, MANY offers, but I've kept faithful. Even with all the offers.

Or

☐ **TRUMP:** People would have been forgiving [of Bill Clinton] if he'd had an affair with a really beautiful woman of sophistication.

31.

☐ **TRUMP:** Why does Bush take forever to get off Air Force 1? Don't you have a country to run?!

Or

☐ **TRUMP:** The way President Obama runs down the stairs of Air Force 1, hopping & bobbing all the way, so inelegant and unpresidential. Do not fall!

32.

☐ **TRUMP:** Winston Churchill was an unbelievable leader. Why? He was born with a speech impediment, he had all sorts of problems, he certainly wasn't a handsome man, and, yet, he was a great leader. Why was he a great leader? Nobody knows.

Or

☐ **TRUMP:** Winston Churchill was in the right place at the right time. Of course people were gonna love him. He got the United Kingdom through the war. Was he actually a good leader? No. Was he a confused and strange looking old man? Yes.

❏ **TRUMP:** I think I would probably get along with . . . [Vladimir Putin] very well, and I don't think you'd be having the kind of problems that you're having right now.
Or

❏ **TRUMP:** I make enemies faster than I make friends. You need time for trust in friendships. Putin does not have my trust and so right now, he's my enemy.

34.

❏ **TRUMP:** This is the end of Bush and his administration. Loads of idiots and phoneys leading us into Iraq. Trust me, this is the end for him.
Or

❏ **TRUMP:** Saddam Hussein is gonna be like a nice guy compared to the one who's taking over Iraq. Somebody will take over Iraq, whether we're there or not.

35.

❏ **TRUMP:** Oprah, I love Oprah. Oprah would always be my first choice [of Vice President].
Or

❏ **TRUMP:** My first choice [of Vice President] would be Mike Tyson. Love that guy.

36.

❏ **TRUMP:** I never attacked him [Rand Paul] on his looks, and believe me, there's plenty of subject matter right there.
Or

❏ **TRUMP:** I wouldn't attack Jimmy Fallon's looks. I wouldn't. But if I was going to, I'd say he looks like a frog.

37.

☐ **TRUMP:** [John McCain is] not a war hero. He's a war hero – he's a war hero 'cause he was captured. I like people that weren't captured, OK, I hate to tell you.

Or

☐ **TRUMP:** We need to help Berghdal . . , He is a US citizen and was fighting for our country. Taken by the Taliban for FIVE YEARS. Sort this out Obama!!

38.

☐ **TRUMP:** Rosie O'Donnell won a daytime Emmy? Do people not have eyes or ears? Who are the suckers that vote on this ridiculous awards programme?

Or

☐ **TRUMP:** Well, Rosie O'Donnell's disgusting, both inside and out. You take look at her, she's a slob. She talks like a truck driver.

39.

☐ **TRUMP:** Probably I'll sue her, because it would be fun. I'd like to take some money out of her fat-ass pockets.

Or

☐ **TRUMP:** I like to sue people. I've got the money, I've got the money to sue and not even worry about it. Because I always win. Especially against idiots.

40.

☐ **TRUMP:** I promise you that I'm much smarter than Jonathan Lebowitz – I mean John Stewart @TheDailyShow. Who, by the way, is totally overrated.

Or

☐ **TRUMP:** No matter what you do, it always comes with an extra layer of gleeful cruelty and dickishness.

❏ **TRUMP:** Lebron James was just interviewed by the dumbest man on television, Don Lemon. He made Lebron look smart, which isn't easy to do.

Or

❏ **TRUMP:** I know more about sport than most people. People don't expect that. But I do, I know loads about sport and I know that Lebron James is overrated. His face is everywhere at the moment, I can't escape it!

42.

❏ **TRUMP:** Alec Baldwin, whose dying mediocre career was saved by his impersonation of me on SNL, now says playing DJT was agony for him. Alex, it was also agony for those who were forced to watch. You were terrible. Bring back Darrell Hammond, much funnier and a far greater talent!

Or

❏ **TRUMP:** Alec Baldwin's impersonation of me isn't even offensive. It's just plain stupid. I'd do a better impression of him by speaking in a monotone voice and acting in some really terrible films. He's just not funny.

43.

❏ **TRUMP:** While Putin is scheming and beaming on how to take over the World, President Obama is watching March Madness (basketball)!

Or

❏ **TRUMP:** While Kim Jong-un has his finger on the nuclear button, the Democrats are discussing ridiculous 'Obamacare'. Sort your priorities out!

☐ **TRUMP:** Joe Biden got tongue tied over the weekend when he was unable to properly deliver a very simple line about his decision to run for President. Get used to it, another low IQ individual!

Or

☐ **TRUMP:** So glad Joe Biden is running for president, I look great next to him and he's so pathetic America will never choose them to lead. Another one will bite the dust!

45.

☐ **TRUMP:** Golf is a great, great sport. It clears the mind; it keeps you active and real men play golf. It's a real man's sport. That's probably why I play it.

Or

☐ **TRUMP:** Can you believe that, with all of the problems and difficulties facing the US, President Obama spent the day playing golf?

46.

☐ **TRUMP:** I think Eminem is fantastic, and most people think I wouldn't like Eminem.

Or

☐ **TRUMP:** Eminem thinks he can rap, but trust me I'm way better with words. I'm better with words than most rappers. Look how popular I am on Twitter.

47.

☐ **TRUMP:** If crazy @megynkelly didn't cover me so much on her terrible show, her ratings would totally tank. She is so average in so many ways!

Or

☐ **TRUMP:** Fox started going downhill when @megynkelly started her show. She's attractive, yes. But a terrible host.

❑ **TRUMP:** You could see there was blood coming out of her eyes, blood coming out of her wherever.

Or

❑ **TRUMP:** She was mad. Really mad. That's normal for women though.

49.

❑ **TRUMP:** I am a defender of @MileyCyrus, who I think is a good person (and not because she stays at my hotels), but last night's outfit must go!

Or

❑ **TRUMP:** No @mileycyrus. You've changed. America's sweetheart to rubbing against that moron Robin Thick at the VMAs. What happened to you? Go to church!

50.

❑ **TRUMP:** Sarah Jessica Parker voted 'unsexiest woman alive' – I agree.

Or

❑ **TRUMP:** I had a role on Sex and the City (probably the best scene they've done) and I wouldn't say no to @KimCattrall

THE ANSWERS

1.

TRUMP: If Obama resigns from office NOW, thereby doing a great service to the country- I will give him free lifetime golf at any of my courses![57]

Or

 TRUMP: If Hillary wins, she can stay in Trump Tower for free for the rest of her life. That's a promise. That's how much I know she won't win.

I suppose we never got to find out whether this was true or not...

2.

 TRUMP: Obama trying to woo us all by singing foolishly at a formal event- what a travesty!

Or

TRUMP: Why is Obama playing basketball today? That is why our country is in trouble![58]

Trump frequently criticised Obama for taking time off and having fun, when he has actually taken three times as much holiday as Obama did.[59]

---

57 Twitter, 11 September 2014
58 Twitter, 6 November 2012
59 https://www.independent.co.uk/news/world-0/us-politics/donald-trump-barack-obama-holiday-us-president-golf-bedminster-new-jersey-vacation-mar-a-lago-a7876256.html

3.

 TRUMP: If Hillary Clinton can't satisfy her husband what makes her think she can satisfy America?[60]

Or

 TRUMP: Hillary's the least qualified person I know who could be president, @AlecBaldwin would do a better job and that's saying something.

Trump let loose on Hillary Clinton a great many times during his election campaign, but this one is a particular gem.

4.

 TRUMP: Germany's, like, sitting back silent collecting money and making a fortune with probably the greatest leader in the world today, Merkel.[61]

Or

 TRUMP: Merkel is a leader I can't have a proper conversation with because she doesn't understand what it is to need a wall.

Years back Trump was complimentary about Angela Merkel's running of Germany. He's changed his tune somewhat since, but still admitted that he has 'unbelievable chemistry'[62] with her in 2017.

60   Twitter, 16 April 2015
61   Interview with *TIME* magazine, 18 August 2015
62   Interview with the Associated Press, 23 April 2017

5.

TRUMP: If Ivanka weren't my daughter, perhaps I'd be dating her. Is that terrible?[63]

Or

FAKE **TRUMP:** Ivanka is the cleverest of my children, just the cleverest. Eric tries but what you gonna do.

Yes, Donald, it is.

6.

FAKE **TRUMP:** Sad face for @katyperry, you have a big heart and Russell Brand looked good next to you.

Or

TRUMP: @katyperry Katy, what the hell were you thinking when you married loser Russell Brand. There is a guy who has got nothing going, a waste! [64]

Trump making it clear here that he is not a Russell Brand fan (he's actually tweeted a few times about his dislike for Russell). Not sure why he is so interested in Katy Perry's love life though.

---

63   *The View*, 6 March 2006
64   Twitter, 16 October 2014

7

TRUMP: Meryl Streep, one of the most over-rated actresses in Hollywood, doesn't know me but attacked last night at the Golden Globes. She is a . . .[65]

Or

FAKE **TRUMP:** Meryl Streep tried to offend me last night at the Golden Globes. I was more offended by her 'acting' in Into the Woods.

Yes, Meryl Streep quite famously called Donald Trump out at the Golden Globes saying 'Disrespect invites disrespect. Violence incites violence. And when the powerful use their position to bully others, we all lose.'[66]

8.

TRUMP: Obama is, without question the WORST EVER president. I predict he will now do something really bad and totally stupid to show manhood! [67]

Or

FAKE **TRUMP:** Everyone saying we were too late to help New Orleans after Katrina – I actually think Bush has done a great job. And that's coming from me.

Trump, if you don't have anything nice to say . . .

---

65   Twitter, 9 January 2017
66   https://edition.cnn.com/2019/01/03/entertainment/meryl-streep-golden-globes/index.html
67   Twitter, 5 June 2014

9.

TRUMP: Why would Kim Jong-un insult me by calling me 'old,' when I would NEVER call him 'short and fat?' Oh well, I try so hard to be his friend - and maybe someday that will happen![68]

Or

 TRUMP: Putin is a strong leader, we could learn a lot from him. We are not best friends, but I'd like to be his friend. A friendship where I would always get what I want.

A very mature tweet here from Donald.

10.

 TRUMP: My son is handsome, so handsome. He gets his looks from his father. I hope he looks this good when he is my age.

Or

 TRUMP: Every guy in the country wants to go out with my daughter[69]

Trump is such a proud dad.

11.

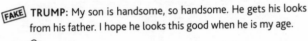 **TRUMP:** How amazing, the State Health Director who verified copies of Obama's "birth certificate" died in plane crash today. All others lived[70]

Or

 TRUMP: People won't want a president that's not American born and bred – it's actually, you know, illegal to have one. That's why I called Obama's into question, it's called clever politic tactics.

Donald Trump, on various occasions, has expressed doubts that Obama was born in the United States (Birtherism).

---

68 Twitter, 11 November 2017
69 *New York* magazine, 13 December 2004
70 Twitter, 12 December 2013

12.

 TRUMP: Everyone knows I am right that Robert Pattinson should dump Kristen Stewart. In a couple of years, he will thank me. Be smart, Robert. [71]

Or

FAKE **TRUMP:** Robert Pattinson and Kristen Stewart make a fantastic couple. In Twilight and outside of Twilight. I'm a fan of the Twilight franchise, a bit fan.

Trump is an expert judge of the private love lives of celebrities.

13.

FAKE **TRUMP:** Kim Kardashian is the hottest one. She's not my type, but she is definitely the hottest one.

Or

 TRUMP: In the old days, they'd say she's [Kim Kardashian] got a bad body.[72]

Trump probably wouldn't be tweeting this nowadays, considering he is currently best mates with Kim Kardashian's husband, Kanye West.

14.

FAKE **TRUMP:** I have nothing to say about her [Cher]. Sonny was the talented one. I think she knows that.

Or

 TRUMP: Cher is somewhat of a loser. She's lonely. She's unhappy. She's very miserable[73]

Cher has always been quite open about her dislike of Trump, once saying 'I just think he's a f---ing idiot.'[74]

---

71 Twitter, 22 October 2012
72 *The Howard Stern Show*, 17 June 2014
73 *On the Record with Greta Van Susteren*, 14 May 2012
74 https://www.billboard.com/articles/news/7486865/cher-donald-trump-
    -rally-video

15.

 TRUMP: @arianahuff is unattractive both inside and out. I fully understand why her former husband left her for a man- he made a good decision[75]

Or

 TRUMP: @Jeffreyzucker, president of CNN is a mess. His looks are terrible, I mean terrible. I don't want to sound like a mean person, but his looks are really terrible.

Trump has voiced a lot of opinions about Ariana Huffington, but this might be the meanest.

16.

 TRUMP: Barney Frank looked disgusting- nipples protruding- in his blue shirt before congress. Very very disrespectful.[76]

Or

 TRUMP: Barney Frank's too-tight trousers were embarrassing. I don't want to see THAT thank you very much. He is a professional . . . so rude.

Because Trump has never said or done anything disrespectful before . . .

75   Twitter, 28 August 2012
76   Twitter, 21 December 2011

17.

 TRUMP: #JebBush has to like Mexican illegals because of his wife.[77]

Or

FAKE **TRUMP:** Who's worse than George Bush? #JebBush. What an idiot.

Jeb Bush's wife is Mexican-American. But being married to an American makes you very much a legal citizen, so . . .

18.

 TRUMP: The concept of . . . [Hillary Clinton's] listening tour is ridiculous. People want ideas. Do you think Winston Churchill, when he was stopping Hitler, went around listening?[78]

Or

FAKE **TRUMP:** Hillary Clinton has so many secrets now she's finding them hard to juggle. She's not smart enough to juggle them. I don't want to sound controversial, but Hitler had a lot of secrets.

He probably did, yes.

19.

FAKE **TRUMP:** My life is full of phone calls. Too many phone calls. Me having to say no to everyone. I'm so in demand. They all want me but I'm too busy – sorry Jay Leno.

Or

 TRUMP: Jay Leno and his people are constantly calling me to go on his show. My answer is always no because his show sucks. They love my ratings! [79]

---

77   Twitter, 4 April 2015
78   *New York Times*, 19 September 1999
79   Twitter, 5 September 2013

20

FAKE **TRUMP:** I didn't want to say anything because the haters and losers will tell me I'm being politically incorrect. But I don't care- @LadyGaga, it's a no from me.

Or

TRUMP: While @BetteMidler is an extremely unattractive woman, I refuse to say that because I always insist on being politically correct.[80]

Another example of Donald Trump slamming someone who doesn't like him. Bette Midler has been vocal about her dislike for Trump, tweeting 'Maybe Trump is the President we deserve. Maybe we have become so corrupt, amoral, materialistic, greedy, ruthless, manipulative, and such liars, that he really does represent who we really are'[81]

---

80   Twitter, 28 October 2012
81   Twitter, 20 April 2019

21.

CAMERON: I hate both of them [*The Apprentice* and Alan Sugar]. I can't bear Alan Sugar.[82]

Or

TRUMP: Dopey @Lord_Sugar I'm worth $8 billion and you're worth peanuts . . . without my show nobody would even know who you are.[83]

Trump has ranted a few times on Twitter about Lord Sugar, and David Cameron said the first one in 2009. Can't we just all get along?! Well, as it turns out, the latter two do now: Alan Sugar ended up working for David Cameron in 2016.[84]

22.

TRUMP: @BarackObama hard at work yesterday shooting a marshmallow cannon in the WH East Room while our country burns.[85]

Or

 FAKE **TRUMP:** @HillaryClinton has spent most of her campaign tour shopping rather than working like me – we can't have a president who only shops!

Trump doesn't like to exaggerate.
We get it already, you don't think Obama's good!

---

82 https://www.independent.co.uk/news/people/alan-lord-sugar-appointed-as-david-camerons-enterprise-tsar-a7047676.html
83 Twitter, 7 December 2012
84 https://www.independent.co.uk/news/people/alan-lord-sugar-appointed-as-david-camerons-enterprise-tsar-a7047676.html
85 Twitter, 8 February 2012

23

TRUMP: Hillary's downfall was lying. America does not deserve to be lied to . . . I've never lied in my life. Not once. Not once have I lied and that's the truth. Hillary is lying every day and you can tell. She doesn't look comfortable, she doesn't look stable. I'm the most stable person in the world.

Or

 TRUMP: Actually, throughout my life, my two greatest assets have been mental stability and being, like, really smart. Crooked Hillary Clinton also played these cards very hard and, as everyone knows, went down in flames. I went from VERY successful businessman, to top T.V. Star.[86]

Interestingly, people have been questioning Trump's mental stability for a while now,[87] a lot of it based on his Twitter rampages.

24.

 TRUMP: @AlexSalmond of Scotland may be the dumbest leader of the free world. I can't imagine that anyone wants him in office.[88]

Or

 TRUMP: Stupid @AlexSalmond sitting there in Scotland not having a clue what he is doing. Someone give the guy some tips.

---

86   Twitter, 6 January 2018
87   https://www.bbc.co.uk/news/world-us-canada-42580762
88   Twitter, 29 October 2013

25.

FAKE TRUMP: No no no. I refuse to watch Family Guy. Stupid TV show with stupid characters. Written by a bunch of people with no brains and a gross sense of humour

Or

 TRUMP: Just tried watching Modern Family - written by a moron, really boring. Writer has the mind of a very dumb and backward child. Sorry Danny!"[89]

Well it's not for everyone.

26.

 TRUMP: Why does @BarackObama always have to rely on teleprompters?[90]

Or

TRUMP: Bad performance by Crooked Hillary Clinton! Reading poorly from the teleprompter! She doesn't even look presidential! [91]

Yes Trump said both of these. He also uses a teleprompter a lot, so . . . [92]

27.

 TRUMP: @cher – I don't wear a 'rug' – it's mine. And I promise not to talk about your massive plastic surgeries that didn't work.[93]

Or

FAKE TRUMP: I don't give a s*** what @cardib says about my hair. It looks better than her wig. At least mine is ALL MINE.

Well that clears that up.

---

89 Twitter, 13 June 2013
90 Twitter, 19 March 2012
91 Twitter, 2 June 2016
92 https://www.politico.com/story/2019/02/04/trump-state-of-the-union-2019-preview-1144760
93 Twitter, 13 November 2012

28.

TRUMP: Great personality and very smart [Kim Jong-un]. Good combination . . . learned he's a very talented man. I also learned that he loves his country very much.[94]

Or

 TRUMP: Kim Jong-un of North Korea is crazy. He's just crazy. He needs better security!

Yes, Donald Trump said talking with the North Korean leader went well and gushed about his personality. Was this before or after they threatened each other with nuclear weapons?

29.

 TRUMP: The media is a parasite. Spreading FAKE NEWS wherever they go. Don't believe a word of it, not one word. The greatest thing that I have ever done is have THIS REALISATION.

Or

 TRUMP: The media is really the word – I think one of the greatest of all terms I've come up with is fake. I guess other people have used it perhaps over the years, but I've never noticed it.[95]

You heard it from the man himself: the greatest term he has ever come up with is 'fake'.

94   Voice of America, 2018
95   Interview with Mike Huckabee on 7 October 2017

30.

 TRUMP: The man [Bill Clinton] couldn't even be loyal to his wife. I've had many offers, trust me, MANY offers, but I've kept faithful. Even with all the offers.

Or

 TRUMP: People would have been forgiving [of Bill Clinton] if he'd had an affair with a really beautiful woman of sophistication.[96]

Would they, though?

31.

 TRUMP: Why does Bush take forever to get off Air Force 1? Don't you have a country to run?

Or

 TRUMP: The way President Obama runs down the stairs of Air Force 1, hopping & bobbing all the way, so inelegant and unpresidential. Do not fall![97]

He can't do anything right!

32.

 TRUMP: Winston Churchill was an unbelievable leader. Why? He was born with a speech impediment, he had all sorts of problems, he certainly wasn't a handsome man, and, yet, he was a great leader. Why was he a great leader? Nobody knows.[98]

Or

 TRUMP: Winston Churchill was in the right place at the right time. Of course people were gonna love him. He got the United Kingdom through the war. Was he actually a good leader? No. Was he a confused and strange looking old man? Yes.

Hang on, explain that again?

---

96   *New York Times*, 19 September 1999
97   Twitter, 22 April 2014
98   *Larry King Live*, 10 August 1999

33

TRUMP: I think I would probably get along with . . . [Vladimir Putin] very well, and I don't think you'd be having the kind of problems that you're having right now[99]

Or

 FAKE **TRUMP:** I make enemies faster than I make friends. You need time for trust in friendships. Putin does not have my trust and so right now, he's my enemy

#trumpputin

34.

 FAKE **TRUMP:** This is the end of Bush and his administration. Loads of idiots and phoneys leading us into Iraq. Trust me, this is the end for him.

Or

 TRUMP: Saddam Hussein is gonna be like a nice guy compared to the one who's taking over Iraq. Somebody will take over Iraq, whether we're there or not.[100]

Is this actually one of his more insightful comments? We can't tell anymore.

35.

 TRUMP: Oprah, I love Oprah. Oprah would always be my first choice [of Vice President].[101]

Or

 FAKE **TRUMP:** My first choice [of Vice President] would be Mike Tyson. Love that guy.

Sorry Mike Pence!

---

99 *Face the Nation*, 10 November 2015
100 *The Big Idea with Donny Deutsch*, 2006
101 *Larry King Live*, 10 August 1999

36.

TRUMP: I never attacked him [Rand Paul] on his looks, and believe me, there's plenty of subject matter right there.[102]

Or

FAKE TRUMP: I wouldn't attack Jimmy Fallon's looks. I wouldn't. But if I was going to, I'd say he looks like a frog.

So subtle, Donald.

37.

TRUMP: [John McCain is] not a war hero. He's a war hero – he's a war hero 'cause he was captured. I like people that weren't captured, OK, I hate to tell you.[103]

Or

FAKE TRUMP: We need to help Berghdal . . . He is a US citizen and was fighting for our country. Taken by the Taliban for FIVE YEARS. Sort this out Obama!!

Best way of not being captured? Don't fight – as Trump knows.

38.

FAKE TRUMP: Rosie O'Donnell won a daytime Emmy? Do people not have eyes or ears? Who are the suckers that vote on this ridiculous awards programme?

Or

TRUMP: Well, Rosie O'Donnell's disgusting, both inside and out. You take look at her, she's a slob. She talks like a truck driver.[104]

Trump rants about Rosie O'Donnell a lot on Twitter and they have been feuding since 2008 when she described Trump as a 'snake-oil salesman on Little House on the Prairie'.[105]

---

102   CNN Republican debate, 16 September 2015
103   Iowa Family Leadership Summit, 18 July 2015
104   *Entertainment Tonight*, 21 December 2006
105   https://edition.cnn.com/2015/08/07/politics/donald-trump-rosie-odonnell-feud/index.html

TRUMP: Probably I'll sue her, because it would be fun. I'd like to take some money out of her fat-ass pockets.[106]

Or

 FAKE **TRUMP:** I like to sue people. I've got the money, I've got the money to sue and not even worry about it. Because I always win. Especially against idiots.

Talking about Rosie O'Donnell again.

 TRUMP: I promise you that I'm much smarter than Jonathan Lebowitz – I mean John Stewart @TheDailyShow. Who, by the way, is totally overrated.[107]

Or

 FAKE **TRUMP:** No matter what you do, it always comes with an extra layer of gleeful cruelty and dickishness[108]

The second of these is a quote from Jon Stewart about Trump. Trump has also said he had never made fun of Jon Stewart's last name (when people called him out for antiSemitism)

---

106 *Entertainment Tonight*, 21 December 2006
107 Twitter, 24 April 2013
108 Jon Stewart on *The Late Show*, June 2018

41.

 TRUMP: Lebron James was just interviewed by the dumbest man on television, Don Lemon. He made Lebron look smart, which isn't easy to do.[109]

Or

 TRUMP: I know more about sport than most people. People don't expect that. But I do, I know loads about sport and I know that Lebron James is overrated. His face is everywhere at the moment, I can't escape it!

Poor Don.

42.

 TRUMP: Alec Baldwin, whose dying mediocre career was saved by his impersonation of me on SNL, now says playing DJT was agony for him. Alex, it was also agony for those who were forced to watch. You were terrible. Bring back Darrell Hammond, much funnier and a far greater talent! [110]

Or

 TRUMP: Alec Baldwin's impersonation of me isn't even offensive. It's just plain stupid. I'd do a better impression of him by speaking in a monotone voice and acting in some really terrible films. He's just not funny.

Mediocre career? Has he not seen Boss Baby? Alec said that although it was agony, he would still play Trump again.[111]

---

109 Twitter, 4 August 2018
110 Twitter, 2 March 2018
111 https://www.washingtonpost.com/

43

TRUMP: While Putin is scheming and beaming on how to take over the World, President Obama is watching March Madness (basketball)![112]

Or

 TRUMP: While Kim Jong-un has his finger on the nuclear button, the Democrats are discussing ridiculous 'Obamacare'. Sort your priorities out!

What does 'beaming' mean again?

44.

 TRUMP: Joe Biden got tongue tied over the weekend when he was unable to properly deliver a very simple line about his decision to run for President. Get used to it, another low IQ individual![113]

Or

 TRUMP: So glad Joe Biden is running for president, I look great next to him and he's so pathetic America will never choose them to lead. Another one will bite the dust!

Anyone else really want to know Trump's IQ?

---

112   Twitter, 20 March 2014
113   Twitter, 18 March 2019

45.

FAKE **TRUMP:** Golf is a great, great sport. It clears the mind; it keeps you active and real men play golf. It's a real man's sport. That's probably why I play it.

Or

 TRUMP: Can you believe that, with all of the problems and difficulties facing the US, President Obama spent the day playing golf.[114]

According to the internet, Trump has been to Mar-a-Lago to play golf an estimated 174 times since becoming president.[115]

46.

 TRUMP: I think Eminem is fantastic, and most people think I wouldn't like Eminem.[116]

Or

FAKE **TRUMP:** Eminem thinks he can rap, but trust me I'm way better with words. I'm better with words than most rappers. Look how popular I am on Twitter.

In Eminem's record 'The Ringer', he raps about Trump: 'I empathise with the people this evil serpent sold the dream to that he's deserted.'[117]

114 Twitter, 13 October 2014
115 https://trumpgolfcount.com/
116 *Playboy* interview, October 2004
117 https://www.theguardian.com/music/2018/aug/31/eminem-donald-trump-surprise-album-kamikaze

47

TRUMP: If crazy @megynkelly didn't cover me so much on her terrible show, her ratings would totally tank. She is so average in so many ways![118]

Or

 TRUMP: Fox started going downhill when @megynkelly started her show. She's attractive, yes. But a terrible host.

This was said about Megyn Kelly who is another person who has experienced firey insults from Donald Trump after calling him out for his comments about women.

48.

 TRUMP: You could see there was blood coming out of her eyes, blood coming out of her wherever.[119]

Or

 TRUMP: She was mad. Really mad. That's normal for women though.

This tweet caused controversy and Donald quickly backtracked and tweeted 'Re Megyn Kelly quote: "you could see there was blood coming out of her eyes, blood coming out of her wherever" (NOSE). Just got on w/thought.'[120]

---

118   Twitter, 19 March 2016
119   *CNN Tonight*, 6 July 2015
120   Twitter, 8 August 2015

49.

TRUMP: I am a defender of @MileyCyrus, who I think is a good person (and not because she stays at my hotels), but last night's outfit must go! [121]

Or

FAKE **TRUMP:** No @mileycyrus. You've changed. America's sweetheart to rubbing against that moron Robin Thick, at the VMAs. What happened to you? Go to church!

Miley Cyrus needs Donald's personal styling tips.

50.

TRUMP: Sarah Jessica Parker voted 'unsexiest woman alive' – I agree.[122]

Or

FAKE **TRUMP:** I had a role on Sex and the City (probably the best scene they've done) and trust me, I wouldn't say no to @KimCattrall.

Another comment on a woman's looks? We're disappointed, Donald.

---

121   Twitter, 23 September 2013
122   Twitter, 26 October 2012

WORLD ISSUES

THE QUESTIONS

1.

❑ **TRUMP:** Climate change has happened since dinosaur times, it's happened since cave men walked the earth. And they didn't have cars in the Ice Age.

Or

❑ **TRUMP:** It's really cold outside, they are calling it a major freeze, weeks ahead of normal. Man, we could use a big fat dose of global warming!

2.

❑ **TRUMP:** People don't know this about Iraq but they have one of the largest oil reserves in the world . . . I always said take the oil.

Or

❑ **TRUMP:** The new evidence is that billions of barrels' worth of oil is under Antarctica, why do scientists whine about melting of ice caps . . . I will pay for the drills.

3.

❑ **TRUMP:** The button for nuclear weapons is on my desk. This is not blackmail but reality.

Or

❑ **TRUMP:** I too have a Nuclear Button, but it is a much bigger & more powerful one than his, and my Button works!

❑ **WORLD LEADER:** . . . .

4

☐ **TRUMP:** We're rounding 'em up in a very humane way, in a very nice way.

Or

☐ **TRUMP:** We need to get bad people out of this country and keep the good people in. It's that simple.

5.

☐ **TRUMP:** This could be the greatest Trojan horse. This could make the Trojan horse look like peanuts if these people turned out to be a lot of ISIS.

Or

☐ **TRUMP:** It's gonna be like that film, Ocean's Eleven. They're all gonna sneak in right under our noses and take stuff from us. That's what ISIS do.

6.

☐ **TRUMP:** It will be a real wall. It'll be a wall that works. It'll actually be a wall that will look good, believe it or not.

Or

☐ **TRUMP:** Some people are saying we don't need a wall. Clearly they don't see what is happening right in front of their eyes. We need a wall.

7.

☐ **TRUMP:** If I could live anywhere else it would probably be Russia. Don't get me wrong, I love America, but they have strong leadership over there.

Or

☐ **TRUMP:** I know the Chinese. I've made a lot of money with the Chinese. I understand the Chinese mind.

8

❑ **TRUMP:** Windmills are the greatest threat in the US to both bald eagles and golden eagles. Media claims fictional "global warming" is worse.

Or

❑ **TRUMP:** I hate windmills, they look nasty and we don't need 'em. Wake up to the climate change LIE people!

9.

❑ **TRUMP:** They're sending people that have lots of problems, and they're bringing those problems with us. They're bringing drugs. They're bringing crime. They're rapists. And some, I assume, are good people.

Or

❑ **TRUMP:** We are becoming overrun. Overrun. There's too many people and it's affecting decent, hard-working Americans. We have to look after our own people. The people of America. I don't want rapists coming over here.

10.

❑ **TRUMP:** First of all, I love China. The people are great. They buy my apartments for $50 million all the time. How could I dislike 'em right?

Or

❑ **TRUMP:** A lot of my money is Chinese money, I'd say $1 billion. $1 billion of my money is Chinese, but that doesn't mean I have to like 'em, right?

11.

☐ **TRUMP:** I think that I would probably get along with him very well, and I don't think you would be having the kind of problems that you're having right now.
Or

☐ **TRUMP:** It's possible to negotiate with him, to search for compromises. On a personal level he made a very good impression on me.

☐ **WORLD LEADER:** . . . .

12.

☐ **TRUMP:** If you look at Saddam Hussein, he killed terrorists. I'm not saying he was an angel, but this guy killed terrorists.
Or

☐ **TRUMP:** I'm not defending Saddam Hussein but he knows what he wants and he goes out and gets it. Hard-line policies are what America needs right now.

13.

☐ **TRUMP:** Stupid Obama, he is letting ISIS walk all over him. He's so kind to them he might as well join 'em.
Or

☐ **TRUMP:** I have an absolute way of defeating ISIS, and it would be decisive and quick and it would be very beautiful.

14.

☐ **TRUMP:** When you see the other side chopping off heads, waterboarding doesn't sound very severe.

Or

☐ **TRUMP:** The death penalty needs to be in all states, all states. We can't let bad people get away with being bad.

15.

☐ **TRUMP:** The concept of Global warming was created by and for the Chinese in order to make US manufacturing non-competitive.

Or

☐ **TRUMP:** Don't get me wrong, I love birds and animals, but I'm not worried for them. 'Global warming' is just a big unnecessary fuss.

16.

☐ **TRUMP:** I just don't know why they [Syrian asylum seekers] come over here. I mean in the last war, World War Two or the civil war even, people stayed at home, they fought for their countries, they stuck it out. You don't hear about Americans fleeing. We don't give up.

Or

☐ **TRUMP:** These [Syrian asylum seekers] are physically young, strong men. They look like prime-time soldiers. Now it's probably not true, but where are the women? . . . So, you ask two things. Number one, why aren't they fighting for their country? And number two, I don't want these people coming over here.

17

☐ **TRUMP:** We are a fucking generous country. Too generous, that's the problem. We share our aid [overseas], our people, our land. But guess what? What happened to helping our own? Caring about America? And making America great again!
Or

☐ **TRUMP:** [Overseas] we build a school, we build a road, they blow up the school, we build another school, we build another road, they blow them up, we build again. In the meantime we can't get a fucking school in Brooklyn.

18.

☐ **TRUMP:** The US cannot allow EBOLA-infected people back. People that go to far away places to help out are great – but must suffer the consequences!
Or

☐ **TRUMP:** We need to save the Americans who have been infected by EBOLA! We go over there to help other people, other countries. Countries that aren't helping us. We can't lose any more of our own!

19.

☐ **TRUMP:** Holding a gun is the best feeling in the world.
Or

☐ **TRUMP:** A 'gun free' school is a magnet for bad people.

20.

☐ **TRUMP:** I know my stuff, I'm smart. A quick learner. I learnt politics didn't I? I learnt politics and I'm getting A+ so far.
Or

☐ **TRUMP:** It would take an hour and a half to learn everything there is to learn about missiles . . . I think I know most of it anyway.

21

☐ **TRUMP:** Shaking hands and eye contact is so important in business. Power is built on trust and trust can be made from a simple handshake. I wouldn't hire anyone with a pathetic handshake. Pathetic handshake, pathetic person.

Or

☐ **TRUMP:** Something very important . . . may come out of the Ebola epidemic that will be a very good thing: NO SHAKING HANDS!

22.

☐ **TRUMP:** I don't mind having a big beautiful door in that wall so that people can come into this country legally.

Or

☐ **TRUMP:** My wall will be impenetrable, no one is getting through that wall. No one else has been brave enough to say it, but that's what we need.

23.

☐ **TRUMP:** We'll be fine with the environment. We can leave a little bit, but you can't destroy business.

Or

☐ **TRUMP:** These champagne liberals preaching about the environment. They're preaching about the environment but they don't know what it's like to need money. Business keeps people alive.

24.

☐ **TRUMP:** My favourite animal is a Lion. It's smart. It's top of the food chain. It's powerful and it doesn't have time for your bullshit.

Or

☐ **TRUMP:** Sorry, folks, I'm just not a fan of sharks – and don't worry, they will be around long after we are gone.

25

☐ **TRUMP:** Of course we should have captured Osama Bin Laden long before we did. I pointed him out in my book just BEFORE the attack on the World Trade Center. President Clinton famously missed his shot. We paid Pakistan Billions of Dollars & they never told us he was living there. Fools!

Or

☐ **TRUMP:** Yeah it took us time to capture Osama Bin Laden, but he was a professional, he was stealthy and cunning. We need to do everything we can now to make sure it doesn't happen again. WE need to be stealthy and cunning. Who isn't stealthy and cunning? OBAMA!

26.

☐ **TRUMP:** Brutal and Extended Cold Blast could shatter ALL RECORDS - Whatever happened to Global Warming?

Or

☐ **TRUMP:** IT'S REALLY, REALLY COLD, SO COLD. Stay warm, America.

27.

☐ **TRUMP:** Trust me, I know science better than anyone. People underestimate me, but I know science and I know that weather is weather. I've been right about a lot of things before and I'm right about this

Or

☐ **TRUMP:** The Democrats are trying to belittle the concept of a wall, calling it old fashioned. The fact is there is nothing else that will work, and that has been true for thousands of years. It's like the wheel, there is nothing better. I know tech better than anyone, & technology . . .

28

☐ **TRUMP:** So funny to watch people who have failed for years, they got NOTHING, telling me how to negotiate with North Korea. But thanks anyway!

Or

☐ **TRUMP:** I know how talented I am. I like to think I'm a lone wolf but really you need to surround yourself with the best. Ask advice, that's important. But know your own mind.

29.

☐ **TRUMP:** I WILL DEFEAT ISIS. THEY HAVE BEEN AROUND TOO LONG! What has our leadership been doing? #DrainTheSwamp

Or

☐ **TRUMP:** ISIS will be more powerful than America at this rate. The government need to GET A GRIP. They are RUINING this country.

30.

☐ **TRUMP:** I ate a delicious fish today and I don't care what the environmentalists or the vegans or whatever say. That's bullshit, let me eat my fish.

Or

☐ **TRUMP:** Is there a drought? . . . No, we have plenty of water . . . We shove it out to sea . . . They're shoving it out sea [because environmentalists are] trying to protect a certain kind of 3-inch fish.

31.

☐ **TRUMP:** It's a thing called nuclear weapons and other things like lots of things that are done with uranium including some bad things.

Or

☐ **TRUMP:** Believe me they know we have nuclear weapons but do they believe that we will use them? Do they believe that? We believe them but do they believe us?

THE ANSWERS

1.

TRUMP: Climate change has happened since dinosaur times, it's happened since cave men walked the earth. And they didn't have cars in the Ice Age.

Or

TRUMP: It's really cold outside, they are calling it a major freeze, weeks ahead of normal. Man, we could use a big fat dose of global warming![123]

Well who isn't wistful for climate change?

2.

TRUMP: People don't know this about Iraq but they have one of the largest oil reserves in the world . . . I always said take the oil.[124]

Or

TRUMP: The new evidence is that billions of barrels' worth of oil is under Antarctica, why do scientists whine about melting of ice caps . . . I will pay for the drills.

Trump here describing the war crimes he would have committed had he been in charge of the Iraq war.

---

123   Twitter, 19 October 2015
124   Interview with NBC News, 7 September 2016

3.

 KIM JONG-UN: The button for nuclear weapons is on my desk. This is not blackmail but reality.[125]

Or

 TRUMP: I too have a Nuclear Button, but it is a much bigger & more powerful one than his, and my Button works![126]

Double points if you correctly identified that the first statement was said by Kim Jong-un and that the second was from Trump (who might be compensating for something?).

4.

 TRUMP: We're rounding 'em up in a very humane way, in a very nice way.[127]

Or

 TRUMP: We need to get bad people out of this country and keep the good people in. It's that simple.

This quote caused a lot of controversy, as you can imagine.

125 Kim Jong-Un's New Year address, 2018
126 Twitter, 2 January 2018
127 *60 Minutes*, 27 September 2015

5.

TRUMP: This could be the greatest Trojan horse. This could make the Trojan horse look like peanuts if these people turned out to be a lot of ISIS.[128]

Or

 TRUMP: It's gonna be like that film, Oceans Eleven. They're all gonna sneak in right under our noses and take stuff from us. That's what ISIS do.

Trump on Syrian asylum seekers.

6.

TRUMP: It will be a real wall. It'll be a wall that works. It'll actually be a wall that will look good, believe it or not.[129]

Or

TRUMP: Some people are saying we don't need a wall. Clearly they don't see what is happening right in front of their eyes. We need a wall.

I guess if you're spending $15 billion[130] on a wall, you would expect it to look good.

---

128   *Face the Nation*, 11 October 2015
129   *60 minutes*, 27 September 2015
130   https://www.washingtonpost.com/business/about-that-wall-trump-said-mexico-would-be-paying-for/2018/12/12/118ac778-fe27-11e8-a17e-162b712e8fc2_story.html?utm_term=.61dc70c437ab

7.

FAKE **TRUMP:** If I could live anywhere else it would probably be Russia. Don't get me wrong, I love America, but they have strong leadership over there.

Or

 TRUMP: I know the Chinese. I've made a lot of money with the Chinese. I understand the Chinese mind.[131]

Did you know lots of people in China are making fake Trump tweets for fun?[132] Someone send them this book!

8.

 TRUMP: Windmills are the greatest threat in the US to both bald eagles and golden eagles. Media claims fictional 'global warming' is worse.[133]

Or

FAKE **TRUMP:** I hate windmills, they look nasty and we don't need 'em. Wake up to the climate change LIE people!

Media and thousands of scientists, who consistently show a 97–98 per cent consensus that humans are causing global warming.[134]

·

131   Xinhua, April 2011
132   https://www.scmp.com/news/china/society/article/2065786/chinese-create-fake-trump-tweets-jokes-and-new-year-wishes
133   Twitter, 9 September 2014
134   https://skepticalscience.com/global-warming-scientific-consensus-advanced.htm

9.

TRUMP: They're sending people that have lots of problems, and they're bringing those problems with us. They're bringing drugs. They're bringing crime. They're rapists. And some, I assume, are good people.[135]

Or

 TRUMP: We are becoming overrun. Overrun. There's too many people and it's affecting decent, hard-working Americans. We have to look after our own people. The people of America. I don't want rapists coming over here.

Trump on immigrants. Fun fact: did you know that research has shown that actually young immigrants are much less likely to be involved in criminal activity than their American peers[136]? We're SURE if Trump knew this he would apologise.

10.

TRUMP: First of all, I love China. The people are great. They buy my apartments for $50 million all the time. How could I dislike 'em, right?[137]

Or

 TRUMP: A lot of my money is Chinese money, I'd say $1 billion. $1 billion of my money is Chinese, but that doesn't mean I have to like 'em, right?

An apartment for $50 million?? Is it made out of gold?

---

135 Campaign launch rally, 15 June 2015
136 https://www.vox.com/policy-and-politics/2017/4/3/14624918/the-case-for-immigration
137 Virginia rally, 2016

11.

 TRUMP: I think that I would probably get along with him very well, and I don't think you would be having the kind of problems that you're having right now.[138]

Or

 PUTIN: It's possible to negotiate with him, to search for compromises. On a personal level he made a very good impression on me.[139]

Double points if you guessed that the second quote was from Putin about Trump and the first is from Trump about Putin.

12.

 TRUMP: If you look at Saddam Hussein, he killed terrorists. I'm not saying he was an angel, but this guy killed terrorists.[140]

Or

 TRUMP: I'm not defending Saddam Hussein but he knows what he wants and he goes out and gets it. Hard-line policies are what America needs right now.

I'm not saying he was an angel but . . .

138   *Face the Nation,* 11 October 2015
139   Putin interview, 2018
140   *The Big Idea with Donny Deutsch,* 2006

13.

FAKE TRUMP: Stupid Obama, he is letting ISIS walk all over him. He's so kind to them he might as well join 'em.
Or

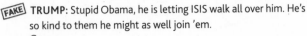 TRUMP: I have an absolute way of defeating ISIS, and it would be decisive and quick and it would be very beautiful.[141]

A beautiful way of . . . defeating a terrorist organisation?

14.

TRUMP: When you see the other side chopping off heads, waterboarding doesn't sound very severe.[142]
Or

FAKE TRUMP: The death penalty needs to be in all states, all states. We can't let bad people get away with being bad.

Waterboarding still sounds pretty severe to us.

15.

TRUMP: The concept of Global warming was created by and for the Chinese in order to make US manufacturing non-competitive.[143]
Or

FAKE TRUMP: Don't get me wrong, I love birds and animals, but I'm not worried for them. 'Global warming' is just a big unnecessary fuss.

And 98 per cent of all scientists in the world are in on it!

---

141 Interview with *The Des Moines Register*, 6 February 2015
142 *This Week with George Stephanopoulos*, 8 February 2016
143 Twitter, 6 November 2012

16

FAKE TRUMP: I just don't know why they [Syrian asylum seekers] come over here. I mean in the last war, World War Two or the civil war even, people stayed at home, they fought for their countries, they stuck it out. You don't hear about Americans fleeing. We don't give up.

Or

TRUMP: These [Syrian asylum seekers] are physically young, strong men. They look like prime-time soldiers. Now it's probably not true, but where are the women? . . . So, you ask two things. Number one, why aren't they fighting for their country? And number two, I don't want these people coming over here.[144]

Number two isn't actually a question though.

17.

FAKE TRUMP: We are a fucking generous country. Too generous, that's the problem. We share our aid [overseas], our people, our land. But guess what? What happened to helping our own? Caring about America? And making America great again!

Or

TRUMP: [Overseas] we build a school, we build a road, they blow up the school, we build another school, we build another road, they blow them up, we build again. In the meantime we can't get a fucking school in Brooklyn.[145]

---

144 *Face the Nation*, 11 October 2015
145 Speech in Las Vegas, 28 April 2011

18.

TRUMP: The US cannot allow EBOLA-infected people back. People that go to far away places to help out are great – but must suffer the consequences!"[146]

Or

TRUMP: We need to save the Americans who have been infected by EBOLA! We go over there to help other people, other countries. Countries that aren't helping us. We can't lose any more of our own!

Seven cases of Ebola were evacuated to the US[147] and two people died.[148]

19.

TRUMP: Holding a gun is the best feeling in the world.

Or

TRUMP: A 'gun free' school is a magnet for bad people.[149]

Trump has been pretty open about his policies on guns, being of the opinion that we need guns to defend ourselves from gunmen.

20.

TRUMP: I know my stuff, I'm smart. A quick learner. I learnt politics didn't I? I learnt politics and I'm getting A+ so far.

Or

TRUMP: It would take an hour and a half to learn everything there is to learn about missiles . . . I think I know most of it anyway.[150]

Any missile experts, don't bother: Donald has it covered.

---

146 Twitter, 9 February 2014
147 'Who are the American Ebola patients?', CNN, 6 October 2014
148 'Nebraska Hospital: Surgeon With Ebola Has Died'. *ABC News,* 17 November 2014.
149 Twitter, 22 February 2018
150 *Washington Post,* 1984

21

TRUMP: Shaking hands and eye contact is so important in business. Power is built on trust and trust can be made from a simple handshake. I wouldn't hire anyone with a pathetic handshake. Pathetic handshake, pathetic person.

Or

 TRUMP: Something very important . . . may come out of the Ebola epidemic that will be a very good thing: NO SHAKING HANDS![151]

Seeing the bright side of a very deadly disease.

22.

 TRUMP: I don't mind having a big beautiful door in that wall so that people can come into this country legally.[152]

Or

 TRUMP: My wall will be impenetrable, no one is getting through that wall. No one else has been brave enough to say it, but that's what we need .

Now let's just get one thing straight: how beautiful is that door going to be?

---

151 Twitter, 4 October 2014
152 *Fox News* Republican debate, 6 August 2015

23.

 TRUMP: We'll be fine with the environment. We can leave a little bit, but you can't destroy business.[153]

Or

FAKE **TRUMP:** These champagne liberals preaching about the environment. They're preaching about the environment but they don't know what it's like to need money. Business keeps people alive.

Pretty sure you need a habitable environment for business to exist.

24.

FAKE **TRUMP:** My favourite animal is a Lion. It's smart. It's top of the food chain. It's powerful and it doesn't have time for your bullshit.

Or

 TRUMP: Sorry, folks, I'm just not a fan of sharks – and don't worry, they will be around long after we are gone.[154]

Trump doesn't like sharks. Glad he let us know that, important information there. Sharks are actually at risk of extinction, according to some scientists so they might not be here for that much longer.[155]

153   *Fox News*, 18 October 2015
154   Twitter, 4 July 2013
155   https://www.theguardian.com/environment/2013/mar/02/sharks-risk-extinction-overfishing-scientists

25

TRUMP: Of course we should have captured Osama Bin Laden long before we did. I pointed him out in my book just BEFORE the attack on the World Trade Center. President Clinton famously missed his shot. We paid Pakistan Billions of Dollars & they never told us he was living there. Fools![156]

Or

 TRUMP: Yeah it took us time to capture Osama Bin Laden, but he was a professional, he was stealthy and cunning. We need to do everything we can now to make sure it doesn't happen again. WE need to be stealthy and cunning. Who isn't stealthy and cunning? OBAMA!

Donald thinking he knows best. Again.

26.

 TRUMP: Brutal and Extended Cold Blast could shatter ALL RECORDS - Whatever happened to Global Warming?[157]

Or

 TRUMP: IT'S REALLY REALLY COLD, SO COLD. Stay warm, America.

Another example here of Trump not understanding the concept of global warming at all.

---

156 Twitter, 19 November 2018
157 Twitter, 22 November 2018

27.

 FAKE TRUMP: Trust me, I know science better than anyone. People underestimate me, but I know science and I know that weather is weather. I've been right about a lot of things before and I'm right about this.

Or

 TRUMP: The Democrats are trying to belittle the concept of a wall, calling it old fashioned. The fact is there is nothing else that will work, and that has been true for thousands of years. It's like the wheel, there is nothing better. I know tech better than anyone, & technology . . . [158]

There you go. Trump knows tech better than you. Are you a technology expert? He still knows better than you.

28.

 TRUMP: So funny to watch people who have failed for years, they got NOTHING, telling me how to negotiate with North Korea. But thanks anyway![159]

Or

 FAKE TRUMP: I know how talented I am. I like to think I'm a lone wolf but really you need to surround yourself with the best. Ask advice, that's important. But know your own mind.

Trump did famously meet the North Korean leader and has uncharacteristically not revealed much about what they talked about.

---

158 Twitter, 21 December 2018
159 Twitter, 24 February 2019

29

TRUMP: I WILL DEFEAT ISIS. THEY HAVE BEEN AROUND TOO LONG! What has our leadership been doing? #DrainTheSwamp[160]

Or

 TRUMP: ISIS will be more powerful than America at this rate. The government need to GET A GRIP. They are RUINING this country.

Fun fact: drain the swamp is a metaphor used by politicians since the 80's who have accused each other of corruption.

30.

 TRUMP: I ate a delicious fish today and I don't care what the environmentalists or the vegans or whatever say. That's bullshit, let me eat my fish.

Or

 TRUMP: Is there a drought? . . . No, we have plenty of water . . . We shove it out to sea . . . They're shoving it out sea [because environmentalists are] trying to protect a certain kind of 3-inch fish.[161]

The three inch fish that he is referring to is an endangered species. But he doesn't like sharks, so maybe he doesn't like fish either?

---

160 Twitter, 19 October 2016
161 Rally in Fresno, 27 May 2016

TRUMP: It's a thing called nuclear weapons and other things like lots of things that are done with uranium including some bad things.[162]

Or

FAKE **TRUMP:** Believe me they know we have nuclear weapons but do they believe that we will use them? Do they believe that? We believe them but to they believe us?

THINGS!

---

162   White House press conference, February 2017

GENERAL WISDOM

THE QUESTIONS

1.

☐ **TRUMP:** My motto is 'Hire the best people, and don't trust them'.

Or

☐ **TRUMP:** Surround yourself with people you can trust.

2.

☐ **TRUMP:** I have never seen a thin person drinking Diet Coke.

Or

☐ **TRUMP:** Some people are just plain stupid, not me, but some people.

3.

☐ **TRUMP:** Certain guys tell me they want women of substance, not beautiful models. It just means they can't get beautiful models.

Or

☐ **TRUMP:** Let's be honest, you wanna go out with someone, you are thinking about going to bed with them. You are thinking about their looks.

4.

☐ **TRUMP:** I love my kids, but you don't get successful by spending time with your children.

Or

☐ **TRUMP:** I won't do anything to take care of them. I'll supply funds and she'll take care of the kids. It's not like I'm gonna be walking the kids down Central Park.

5.

☐ **TRUMP:** Every time I speak of the haters and losers I do so with great love and affection. They cannot help the fact that they were born fucked up!

Or

☐ **TRUMP:** Good morning haters and losers! Another day of me being successful and you being highly irrelevant.

6.

☐ **TRUMP:** These anti-vaxxers are crazy! I care so much about my kids' safety, I'd pump them with everything under the sun, if that's what it took.

Or

☐ **TRUMP:** Healthy young child goes to doctor, gets pumped with massive shot of many vaccines, doesn't feel good and changes – AUTISM. Many such cases!

7.

☐ **TRUMP:** When you're in a fight with a bully, always throw the first punch – and don't telegraph it – hit hard and hit fast!

Or

☐ **TRUMP:** Nothing good comes from throwing the first punch. Kill them with kindness and use your words. I always use my words and it works.

8.

☐ **TRUMP:** Those people at Charlie Hebdo should have listened to me. They needed some business advice and trust me, if they had been doing business better, this wouldn't have happened.

Or

☐ **TRUMP:** If the morons who killed all of those people at Charlie Hebdo would have just waited, the magazine would have folded – no money, no success!

9.

☐ **TRUMP:** HAPPY NEW YEAR to all my fans out there! Here's my advice: dare to dream and the dreams that you wish will come true.

Or

☐ **TRUMP:** To EVERYONE, including all haters and losers, HAPPY NEW YEAR. Work hard, be smart and always remember, WINNING TAKES CARE OF EVERYTHING!

10.

☐ **TRUMP:** Remember, new 'environment friendly' lightbulbs can cause cancer. Be careful – the idiots who came up with this stuff don't care.

Or

☐ **TRUMP:** Remember folks, new Apple Airpods can cause cancer. People aren't talking about it and they should be.

11.

☐ **TRUMP:** You don't need an ego to be successful . . . but it helps, big time.

Or

☐ **TRUMP:** Show me someone without an ego, and I'll show you a loser.

12.

☐ **TRUMP:** Being politically correct is really hard and doesn't make any sense. So hard. I don't want to be politically correct and I shouldn't have to be just 'cause I'm a politician.

Or

☐ **TRUMP:** I think the big problem this country has is being politically correct. I've been challenged by so many people and I don't, frankly, have time for total political correctness.

☐ **TRUMP:** [The media] are constantly writing stories about me and about how women throw themselves at me and they're right.

Or

☐ **TRUMP:** You know, it doesn't really matter what [the media] write as long as you've got a young and beautiful piece of ass.

14.

☐ **TRUMP:** A person who is flat-chested is very hard to be a 10.

Or

☐ **TRUMP:** A person with a large ass is very hard to be a 10.

15.

☐ **TRUMP:** Listen you motherfuckers.

Or

☐ **TRUMP:** Hey up you bastards!

16.

☐ **TRUMP:** Happy CHRISTMAS everyone! I can say it, so I'm gonna. Happy Christmas! All the haters and losers who say we can't say Christmas anymore. It's so stupid. So I'm gonna say it as much as possible – Happy Christmas!!

Or

☐ **TRUMP:** Look at evangelicals, you can't even use the word 'Christmas' anymore, Macy's doesn't use the word 'Christmas.' I mean, you can't even use the word 'Christmas' anymore. And you know with me, it is going to stop, it is going to stop, and they understand that.

17.

☐ **TRUMP:** Let golf be elitist. When I say Aspire, that's a positive word. Let people work hard and aspire to someday be able to play golf.

Or

☐ **TRUMP:** Golf is everyone's sport. It's a sport for everyone. Presidents of the United States, street cleaners, doctors and retail workers. All can play golf!

18.

☐ **TRUMP:** Amazing how the haters & losers keep tweeting the name 'F**kface Von Clownstick' like they are so original & like no one else is doing it . . .

Or

☐ **TRUMP:** Thinking of leaving twitter because of this 'F**kface Von Clownstick' nonsense. Idiots bombarding my twitter. You make it not fun anymore.

19.

☐ **TRUMP:** You have to be careful what you say . . . women are very sensitive.

Or

☐ **TRUMP:** The smart ones act very feminine and needy, but inside they are real killers.

20.

☐ **TRUMP:** O.K., Christmas is over, now we can all go back to the wars of life.

Or

☐ **TRUMP:** Happy Easter! America is still a shithole!

☐ **TRUMP:** Our families, schools, and communities must encourage respect for women.
  Or

☐ **TRUMP:** Grab 'em by the pussy.

22.

☐ **TRUMP:** Get going. Move forward. Aim high. Plan for a takeoff. Don't just sit on the runway and hope someone will come along and push the airplane. It simply won't happen. Change your attitude and gain some altitude. Believe me, you'll love it up here.
  Or

☐ **TRUMP:** Sometimes you've just got to jump off a cliff and see if you can fly. So take the risk. Come fly with me.

23.

☐ **TRUMP:** Tiny children are not horses.
  Or

☐ **TRUMP:** Tiny children are like horses.

24.

☐ **TRUMP:** To get anywhere in life, you have to work hard. And if that means giving up some of life's pleasures, then it's worth it. You can have life's pleasures afterwards with all the money you have earned!
  Or

☐ **TRUMP:** If you're interested in 'balancing' work and pleasure, stop trying to balance them. Instead make your work more pleasurable.

25.

☐ **TRUMP:** Think BIG! You are going to be thinking anyway, so think BIG!

Or

☐ **TRUMP:** Every good idea starts small. Start with a small idea and watch it grow.

26.

☐ **TRUMP:** Living your words, walking your talk, and talking your walk.

Or

☐ **TRUMP:** Live your dreams and dream as you live.

THE ANSWERS

1.

TRUMP: My motto is 'Hire the best people, and don't trust them'.[163]

Or

TRUMP: Surround yourself with people you can trust.[164]

Tricked you! These contradictory statements and were both said by Donald Trump, but hey, people are allowed to change their minds, right?

2.

TRUMP: I have never seen a thin person drinking Diet Coke.[165]

Or

FAKE **TRUMP:** Some people are just plain stupid, not me, but some people.

Interesting observation here.

3.

TRUMP: Certain guys tell me they want women of substance, not beautiful models. It just means they can't get beautiful models[166]

Or

FAKE **TRUMP:** Let's be honest, you wanna go out with someone, you are thinking about going to bed with them. You are thinking about their looks.

Where do models with substance fit in this, do you think?

---

163 *Think Big and Kick Ass: In Business and in Life*, 2007
164 *Trump: How to Get Rich*, 2004
165 Twitter, 14 October 2012
166 *New York Times*, 19 September 1999

4.

`FAKE` **TRUMP:** I love my kids, but you don't get successful by spending time with your children.

Or

TRUMP: I won't do anything to take care of them. I'll supply funds and she'll take care of the kids. It's not like I'm gonna be walking the kids down Central Park.[167]

Great parenting tips here from Donald.

5.

TRUMP: Every time I speak of the haters and losers I do so with great love and affection. They cannot help the fact that they were born fucked up![168]

Or

`FAKE` **TRUMP:** Good morning haters and losers! Another day of me being successful and you being highly irrelevant.

So much love and affection, thanks Donald!

---

167   Howard Stern interview, 2005
168   Twitter, 3 May 2013

6.

FAKE **TRUMP:** These anti-vaxxers are crazy! I care so much about my kids' safety, I'd pump them with everything under the sun, if that's what it took.

Or

TRUMP: Healthy young child goes to doctor, gets pumped with massive shot of many vaccines, doesn't feel good and changes – AUTISM. Many such cases! [169]

Trump responded to the controversy after tweets like this, saying 'I am NOT anti-vaccine, but I am against shooting massive doses into tiny children. Spread shots out over time.'[170]

7.

TRUMP: When you're in a fight with a bully, always throw the first punch – and don't telegraph it – hit hard and hit fast![171]

Or

FAKE **TRUMP:** Nothing good comes from throwing the first punch. Kill them with kindness and use your words. I always use my words and it works.

What happened to 'violence is never the answer'?

---

169   Twitter, 28 March 2014
170   Twitter, 29 March 2014
171   Twitter, 2 September 2014

8.

 TRUMP: Those people at Charlie Hebdo should have listened to me. They needed some business advice and trust me, if they had been doing business better, this wouldn't have happened

Or

 TRUMP: If the morons who killed all of those people at Charlie Hebdo would have just waited, the magazine would have folded – no money, no success![172]

Trump weighs in again here and has another answer to solving atrocities . . .

9.

 TRUMP: HAPPY NEW YEAR to all my fans out there! Here's my advice: dare to dream and the dreams that you wish will come true.

Or

 TRUMP: To EVERYONE, including all haters and losers, HAPPY NEW YEAR. Work hard, be smart and always remember, WINNING TAKES CARE OF EVERYTHING![173]

The world makes sense at last!

---

172   Twitter, 14 January 2015
173   Twitter, 31 December 2014

10.

 TRUMP: Remember, new 'environment friendly' lightbulbs can cause cancer. Be careful-- the idiots who came up with this stuff don't care.[174]

Or

 FAKE **TRUMP:** Remember folks, new Apple Airpods can cause cancer. People aren't talking about it and they should be.

Trump appears to despise lots of environmentally friendly things, but this is going quite far . . .

11.

 FAKE **TRUMP:** You don't need an ego to be successful . . . but it helps, big time.

Or

 TRUMP: Show me someone without an ego, and I'll show you a loser.[175]

Trump is not a loser then.

12.

FAKE **TRUMP:** Being politically correct is really hard and doesn't make any sense. So hard. I don't want to be politically correct and I shouldn't have to be just 'cause I'm a politician.

Or

 TRUMP: I think the big problem this country has is being politically correct. I've been challenged by so many people and I don't, frankly, have time for total political correctness.[176]

At least we know Trump lives by his mantras?

---

174 Twitter, 17 October 2012
175 Twitter, 19 July 2012
176 *Fox News* Republican debate, 6 August 2015

13.

 TRUMP: [The media] are constantly writing stories about me and about how women throw themselves at me and they're right.

Or

 TRUMP: You know, it doesn't really matter what [the media] write as long as you've got a young and beautiful piece of ass.[177]

The way Trump talks about women is so empowering.

14.

 TRUMP: A person who is flat-chested is very hard to be a 10.[178]

Or

TRUMP: A person with a large ass is very hard to be a 10.

Another hugely offensive gem here . . .

15.

 TRUMP: Listen you motherfuckers.[179]

Or

TRUMP: Hey up you bastards!

---

177 *Esquire* magazine, 1991
178 Howard Stern, 2005
179 Speech in Las Vegas, 28 April 2011

16.

 TRUMP: Happy CHRISTMAS everyone! I can say it, so I'm gonna. Happy Christmas! All the haters and losers who say we can't say Christmas anymore. It's so stupid. So I'm gonna say it as much as possible – Happy Christmas!!

Or

 TRUMP: Look at evangelicals, you can't even use the word 'Christmas' anymore, Macy's doesn't use the word 'Christmas.' I mean, you can't even use the word 'Christmas' anymore. And you know with me, it is going to stop, it is going to stop, and they understand that.[180]

Really getting the important changes made! Trump rarely says Happy Holidays, always saying 'Merry Christmas'.

17.

 TRUMP: Let golf be elitist. When I say Aspire, that's a positive word. Let people work hard and aspire to someday be able to play golf.[181]

Or

 TRUMP: Golf is everyone's sport. It's a sport for everyone. Presidents of the United States, street cleaners, doctors and retail workers. All can play golf!

180   *Economist*, 9 March 2015
181   *Fortune*, 7 January 2015

18.

 TRUMP: Amazing how the haters & losers keep tweeting the name 'F**kface Von Clownstick' like they are so original & like no one else is doing it . . . [182]

Or

 TRUMP: Thinking of leaving twitter because of this 'F**kface Von Clownstick' nonsense. Idiots bombarding my twitter. You make it not fun anymore.

The Daily Show *responded to this by tweeting 'We seem to have hit a Fuckface Von Nervestick.'[183]*

19.

 TRUMP: You have to be careful what you say . . . women are very sensitive.

Or

 TRUMP: The smart ones act very feminine and needy, but inside they are real killers.[184]

I did NOT know this about women! Scary.

20.

 TRUMP: O.K., Christmas is over, now we can all go back to the wars of life.[185]

Or

TRUMP: Happy Easter! America is still a shithole!

Merry Christmas to you too!

182   Twitter, 3 May 2013
183   *The Daily Show*, Twitter, 3 May 2013
184   *Trump: The Art of the Comeback*, 1997
185   Twitter, 25 December 2013

21.

 TRUMP: Our families, schools, and communities must encourage respect for women.[186]

Or

 TRUMP: Grab 'em by the pussy.[187]

Both Trump. I have no words.

22.

 TRUMP: Get going. Move forward. Aim high. Plan for a takeoff. Don't just sit on the runway and hope someone will come along and push the airplane. It simply won't happen. Change your attitude and gain some altitude. Believe me, you'll love it up here.[188]

Or

FAKE **TRUMP:** Sometimes you've just got to jump off a cliff and see if you can fly. So take the risk. Come fly with me

Actually some quite, dare we say it, inspirational words here from Donald.

23.

 TRUMP: Tiny children are not horses.[189]

Or

FAKE **TRUMP:** Tiny children are like horses.

OK, so this is taken out of context, but it's pretty funny. Trump was taking about vaccinations here again, tweeting "No more massive injections. Tiny children are not horses—one vaccine at a time, over time"[190].

---

186 National Sexual Assault Awareness and Prevention Month, March 2017
187 *Access Hollywood* tape, 2005
188 *Trump: How to Get Rich*, 2004
189 Twitter, 3 September 2014
190 Twitter, 3 September 2014

24.

 TRUMP: To get anywhere in life, you have to work hard. And if that means giving up some of life's pleasures, then it's worth it. You can have life's pleasures afterwards with all the money you have earned!

Or

 TRUMP: If you're interested in 'balancing' work and pleasure, stop trying to balance them. Instead make your work more pleasurable.[191]

Can't really fault him for saying this one.

25.

 TRUMP: Think BIG! You are going to be thinking anyway, so think BIG![192]

Or

 TRUMP: Every good idea starts small. Start with a small idea and watch it grow.

What if all I'm thinking about is lunch? OH HANG ON . . .

26.

 TRUMP: Living your words, walking your talk, and talking your walk.[193]

Or

 TRUMP: Live your dreams and dream as you live.

How do I walk my talk?

---

191 Twitter, 31 December 2014
192 Trump: The Art of the Deal, 1987
193 *Midas Touch: Why Some Entrepreneurs Get Rich – And Why Most Don't*, 2011

THE US OF A

THE QUESTIONS

1.

☐ **TRUMP:** They've overtaken us in so many things – our education, our infrastructure . . . flying into JFK is like coming into a Third World country.

Or

☐ **TRUMP:** We're becoming a Third World country because of our infrastructure . . . You come into LaGuardia Airport, it's like we're in a Third World country.

2.

☐ **TRUMP:** Every country I visit outside the US is a big shithole.

Or

☐ **TRUMP:** Why are we having all these people from shithole countries coming here?

3.

☐ **TRUMP:** I think if this country gets any kinder or gentler, it's literally going to cease to exist.

Or

☐ **TRUMP:** A friend who bullies us is no longer a friend. And since bullies only respond to strength, from now onward, I will be prepared to be much stronger.

☐ **WORLD LEADER:** . . . .

4.

☐ **TRUMP:** America is weak at the moment. Its borders are weak, its leaders are weak, its politicians are weak. It's weak.

Or

☐ **TRUMP:** We need very strong people, because our country is being taken away. It's like candy from a baby.

5.

☐ **TRUMP:** Ladies and gentlemen, I am officially running for president of the United States and we are going to make our country great again.

Or

☐ **TRUMP:** I have no intention of ever running for president.

6.

☐ **TRUMP:** To all the haters and losers – who's winning now?

Or

☐ **TRUMP:** We are going to have so many victories, you will be bored of winning.

7.

☐ **TRUMP:** This election is a total sham and a travesty. We are not a democracy!

Or

☐ **TRUMP:** There is no point voting anymore, your vote means nothing, they'll choose who they want anyway!

8.

- ❏ **TRUMP:** 26,000 unreported sexual assaults in the military – only 238 convictions. What did these geniuses expect when they put men & women together?

  Or

- ❏ **TRUMP:** Sentences for men are 60% higher than women. The 219,000 women currently incarcerated in the United States are getting a pretty good deal.

9.

- ❏ **TRUMP:** I'd like to send best wishes to all of my enemies this Remembrance Sunday.

  Or

- ❏ **TRUMP:** I would like to extend my best wishes to all, even the haters and the losers, on this special date, September 11th.

10.

- ❏ **TRUMP:** I think I could have stopped . . . [September 11] because I have very tough illegal immigration policies and people aren't coming into this country unless they are vetted and vetted properly.

  Or

- ❏ **TRUMP:** I tell you what, I can promise that . . . [September 11] would not have happened on my watch. Someone let the ball drop and America was too gentle. Too gentle.

11.

- ❏ **TRUMP:** Women love me, not just because I am a handsome guy, but because I respect women. I like women.

  Or

- ❏ **TRUMP:** I will be phenomenal to the women. I mean, I want to help women.

❑ **TRUMP:** Hello America. Obama is still spending your money on his free healthcare shambles, what a waste.
Or

❑ **TRUMP:** It's Thursday. How much money did Barack Obama waste today on crony green energy projects?

13.

❑ **TRUMP:** I truly believe that our country has the worst and dumbest negotiators of virtually any country in the world.
Or

❑ **TRUMP:** Is everyone in the Democrat party an idiot? These dummies couldn't run a doughnut shop let alone a country.

14.

❑ **TRUMP:** Our country is in serious trouble. We don't have victories any more. We used to have victories but [now] we don't have them. When was the last time anybody saw us beating, let's say, China, in a trade deal? They kill us. I beat China all the time. All the time.
Or

❑ **TRUMP:** China is doing everything right right now, unlike us [America]. We need take a page out of their book and listen to them. What are they doing? They have strong leadership and are beating us. We are losing, America is losing.

15.

☐ **TRUMP:** My campaign blows Hillary's out of the water. She's drowning. And at the same time, people are listening to me, listening to everything I say because everything I say is solid gold. All the words from my mouth are changing the world.
Or

☐ **TRUMP:** The line of 'Make America great again,' the phrase, that was mine, I came up with it about a year ago, and I kept using it, and everybody's using it, they are all loving it. I don't know, I guess I should copyright it, maybe I have copyrighted it.

16.

☐ **TRUMP:** I know politicians who love women who don't even want to be known for that, because they might lose the gay vote, OK?
Or

☐ **TRUMP:** Women love me because I've always been great with women. Not just one woman. Many women.

17.

☐ **TRUMP:** If I were starting off today, I would love to be a well-educated black, because I believe they do have an actual advantage.
Or

☐ **TRUMP:** I have a great relationship with African Americans, as you possibly have heard. I just have great respect for them. And they like me. I like them.

18

☐ **TRUMP:** I'm going to be bringing back great numbers of jobs from China, from Japan, from India, from Brazil, from so many countries that have been just absolutely stealing our jobs.
Or

☐ **TRUMP:** Our jobs are not safe, not safe. If we are not careful there will be absolutely no jobs in America in a few years' time.

19.

☐ **TRUMP:** No one in the whole of government should be there. They are ALL stupid and ALL dummies and we need fresh blood!
Or

☐ **TRUMP:** We have very stupid people in our country negotiating for us and we have leaders that don't know what they're doing.

20.

☐ **TRUMP:** Hard to believe I've been a politician for three months, right?
Or

☐ **TRUMP:** I'm not sure I'd describe myself as a politician, I don't want to be associated with them.

21.

☐ **TRUMP:** So many people think I will not run for President. Wow, I wonder what the response will be if I do. Even the haters and losers will be happy!
Or

☐ **TRUMP:** I've always wanted to be president, all my life. I've thought – how could I be most successful? Most powerful? I've always wanted to be president and look at me now. WINNER.

22

❑ **TRUMP:** The only reason I would ever become president is for the women. The women and the power. And the white house. Oh yeh, I would like to live there!
Or
❑ **TRUMP:** I won an election, said to be one of the greatest of all time, based on getting out of endless & costly foreign wars & also based on Strong Borders which will keep our Country safe.

23.

❑ **TRUMP:** With a record deficit and $15 trillion in debt, @BarackObama is spending $4 million of our money on his Hawaii vacation. Just plain wrong.
Or
❑ **TRUMP:** Right, I'm off on holiday. Your president needs a break! Work hard play hard! My mind is never off the ball, but I'll take advantage of 'global warming' and get a bit of sunshine.

24.

❑ **TRUMP:** I like to have fun, I'd be a fun president. I like to make jokes, I like to mock the haters and losers. People shouldn't take themselves so seriously.
Or
❑ **TRUMP:** We need a President who isn't a laughing stock to the entire World. We need a truly great leader, a genius at strategy and winning. Respect!

25.

❑ **TRUMP:** Well, if I ever ran for office, I'd do better as a Democrat than a republican.
Or
❑ **TRUMP:** The Democrats are so self-righteous and ANGRY! Loosen up and have some fun. The Country is doing well!

26.

☐ **TRUMP:** No president ever worked harder than me (cleaning up the mess I inherited)!

Or

☐ **TRUMP:** I think being president would be too hard. The country is a mess and even though I think I'd be great, the best even, I'd rather be playing golf.

27.

☐ **TRUMP:** Lets just call them WALLS from now on and stop playing political games! A WALL is a WALL!

Or

☐ **TRUMP:** It would be a kind of fense. A tall fense. A strong fense. Some would call it a wall. Yes, a wall.

28.

☐ **TRUMP:** It's almost like the United States has no President - we are a rudderless ship heading for a major disaster. Good luck everyone!

Or

☐ **TRUMP:** I'm getting America back on track, steering the ship back home. The great ship. And I'm steering it back to so many happier people.

29.

☐ **TRUMP:** This job, it's crazy, it's hard. It takes a certain type of person to do it well, to do it best. Someone smart and someone who can deal with bigness.

Or

☐ **TRUMP:** Well the one thing I would say – and I say this to people – I never realised how big it was. . . So you know, I really just see the bigness of it all.

30.

☐ **TRUMP:** No politician in history – and I say this with great surety – has been treated worse or more unfairly.

Or

☐ **TRUMP:** People love me and most people treat me with respect and admiration. They can see what I am doing for the country. Even those that didn't vote for me. They can see what I'm doing for this country and they love me.

31.

☐ **TRUMP:** 'We build too many walls and not enough bridges.' – Isaac Newton.

Or

☐ **TRUMP:** 'I am who I am.' – Gloria Gaynor.

32.

☐ **TRUMP:** AMERICA IS STILL NOT RESPECTED! MAGA!

Or

☐ **TRUMP:** AMERICA IS RESPECTED AGAIN!

THE ANSWERS

1.

 TRUMP: They've overtaken us in so many things – our education, our infrastructure . . . flying into JFK is like coming into a Third World country.

Or

TRUMP: We're becoming a third-world country because of our infrastructure . . . You come into LaGuardia Airport, it's like we're in a Third World country.[194]

To be fair, LaGuardia airport can be one of the unfriendliest places on the planet and has been ranked the worst in the USA in a 2018 JD Power Survey (JFK Terminal 3 once topped that – in 2012 it was ranked worst in the world by travel website Frommer's). Third World is pushing it though.

2.

 TRUMP: Every country I visit outside the US is a big shithole.

Or

 TRUMP: Why are we having all these people from shithole countries coming here?[195]

As tactful as ever.

---

194 Campaign launch rally, 15 June 2015
195 White House meeting, 11 January 2018

3.

 TRUMP: I think if this country gets any kinder or gentler, it's literally going to cease to exist[196]

Or

 DAVID: A friend who bullies us is no longer a friend. And since bullies only respond to strength, from now onward I will be prepared to be much stronger.[197]

Hats off if you correctly surmised that this was fictional British prime minister David from Love Actually. (We never said they had to be real world leaders.)

4.

  TRUMP: America is weak at the moment. Its borders are weak, its leaders are weak, its politicians are weak. It's weak.

Or

 TRUMP: We need very strong people, because our country is being taken away. It's like candy from a baby.[198]

Who is taking it away again?

---

196 *Playboy*, March 1990
197 *Love Actually*, 2003
198 *The Herd with Colin Cowherd*, 11 February 2015

5.

TRUMP: Ladies and gentlemen, I am officially running for president of the United States and we are going to make our country great again.[199]

Or

TRUMP: I have no intention of ever running for president.[200]

Fooled you! Trump said both of these things, all be it years apart. People can change their minds though, right?

6.

FAKE **TRUMP:** To all the haters and losers – who's winning now?

Or

TRUMP: We are going to have so many victories, you will be bored of winning[201]

Bored now.

7.

TRUMP: This election is a total sham and a travesty. We are not a democracy! [202]

Or

FAKE **TRUMP:** There is no point voting anymore, your vote means nothing, they'll choose who they want anyway!

America was a democracy when Trump won though, right?

---

199   Speech at Trump Tower, 16 June 2015
200   *TIME*, 14 September 1987
201   *New York Times Magazine*, 4 October 2015
202   Twitter, 7 November 2012

8.

 TRUMP: 26,000 unreported sexual assaults in the military- only 238 convictions. What did these geniuses expect when they put men & women together?[203]

Or

FAKE **TRUMP:** Sentences for men are 60% higher than women. The 219,000 women currently incarcerated in the United States are getting a pretty good deal.

I think they probably expected people not to commit sexual assault. Donald says a lot of controversial things but this one is up there.

9.

FAKE **TRUMP:** I'd like to send best wishes to all of my enemies this Remembrance Sunday.

Or

 TRUMP: I would like to extend my best wishes to all, even the haters and the losers, on this special date, September 11th.[204]

A weird time to bring up the haters and the losers, maybe?

---

203   Twitter, 8 May 2013
204   Twitter, 11 September 2013

10.

 TRUMP: I think I could have stopped . . . [September 11] because I have very tough illegal immigration policies and people aren't coming into this country unless they are vetted and vetted properly.[205]

Or

FAKE **TRUMP:** I tell you what, I can promise that . . . [September 11] would not have happened on my watch. Someone let the ball drop and America was too gentle. Too gentle.

Very bold statement.

11.

FAKE **TRUMP:** Women love me, not just because I am a handsome guy, but because I respect women. I like women.

Or

 TRUMP: I will be phenomenal to the women. I mean, I want to help women.[206]

Phenomenal seems like an overstatement here, especially with policies on restricting abortions[207] and access to birth control.[208]

205   *Hannity*, 20 October 2015
206   *Face the Nation*, 8 September 2015
207   https://womendeliver.org/press/donald-trump-reinstating-policy-restricts-abortions/
208   https://www.abc.net.au/news/2019-01-19/donald-trumps-presidency-two-years-shaped-womens-rights-us/10728882

12.

FAKE TRUMP: Hello America. Obama is still spending your money on his free healthcare shambles, what a waste.

Or

 TRUMP: It's Thursday. How much money did Barack Obama waste today on crony green energy projects?[209]

What does crony mean?

13.

 TRUMP: I truly believe that our country has the worst and dumbest negotiators of virtually any country in the world.[210]

Or

FAKE TRUMP: Is everyone in the Democrat party an idiot? These dummies couldn't run a doughnut shop let alone a country.

Fun fact: At the time of writing, 222 of Trump's tweets have the words 'dumb' or 'dummy' in them.

14.

 TRUMP: Our country is in serious trouble. We don't have victories any more. We used to have victories but [now] we don't have them. When was the last time anybody saw us beating, let's say, China, in a trade deal? They kill us. I beat China all the time. All the time.[211]

Or

FAKE TRUMP: China is doing everything right right now, unlike us [America]. We need to take a page out of their book and listen to them. What are they doing? They have strong leadership and are beating us. We are losing, America is losing.

He has a real thing for China, doesn't he.

---

209 Twitter, 18 October 2012
210 Twitter, 28 November 2013
211 Campaign launch rally, 15 June 2015

15.

 FAKE **TRUMP:** My campaign blows Hillary's out of the water. She's drowning. And at the same time, people are listening to me, listening to everything I say because everything I say is solid gold. All the words from my mouth are changing the world.

Or

 TRUMP: The line of 'Make America great again,' the phrase, that was mine, I came up with it about a year ago, and I kept using it, and everybody's using it, they are all loving it. I don't know, I guess I should copyright it, maybe I have copyrighted it.[212]

Ronald Reagan actually used 'Let's Make America Great Again' as one of his campaign slogans.

16.

 TRUMP: I know politicians who love women who don't even want to be known for that, because they might lose the gay vote, OK?[213]

Or

 FAKE **TRUMP:** Women love me because I've always been great with women. Not just one woman. Many women.

I'm not sure the gay population – or women for that matter – are voting based on who they find attractive.

---

212 MyFox New York, March 2015
213 *Playboy*, March 1990

17.

 TRUMP: If I were starting off today, I would love to be a well-educated black, because I believe they do have an actual advantage.[214]

Or

 TRUMP: I have a great relationship with African Americans, as you possibly have heard. I just have great respect for them. And they like me. I like them.[215]

Yep, both of these inappropriate and bigoted quotes are from Donald Trump.

18.

 TRUMP: I'm going to be bringing back great numbers of jobs from China, from Japan, from India, from Brazil, from so many countries that have been just absolutely stealing our jobs.[216]

Or

 TRUMP: Our jobs are not safe, not safe. If we are not careful there will be absolutely no jobs in America in a few years' time.

Stealing jobs and taking them where?

19.

 TRUMP: No one in the whole of government should be there. They are ALL stupid and ALL dummies and we need fresh blood!

Or

 TRUMP: We have very stupid people in our country negotiating for us and we have leaders that don't know what they're doing.[217]

Trump to the rescue!

---

214 *NBC News* interview, 1989
215 *Anderson Cooper 360*, 23 July 2015
216 *Face the Nation*, 11 August 2015
217 Interview with Katy Tur, *NBC News*, 7 August 2015

20

TRUMP: Hard to believe I've been a politician for three months, right?[218]

Or

FAKE **TRUMP:** I'm not sure I'd describe myself as a politician, I don't want to be associated with them.

Some people could have probably believed that.

21.

 TRUMP: So many people think I will not run for President. Wow, I wonder what the response will be if I do. Even the haters and losers will be happy![219]

Or

FAKE **TRUMP:** I've always wanted to be president, all my life. I've thought – how could I be most successful? Most powerful? I've always wanted to be president and look at me now. WINNER.

Actually a lot of people didn't think he would run for president because he often said in the early 90s that it was not something he was interested in.

---

218   South Carolina rally, 19 October 2015
219   Twitter, 24 December 2014

22.

 TRUMP: The only reason I would ever become president is for the women. The women and the power. And the white house. Oh yeh, I would like to live there!

Or

 TRUMP: I won an election, said to be one of the greatest of all time, based on getting out of endless & costly foreign wars & also based on Strong Borders which will keep our Country safe.[220]

He really gives the ampersand a comeback.

23.

 TRUMP: With a record deficit and $15 trillion in debt, @BarackObama is spending $4 million of our money on his Hawaii vacation. Just plain wrong.[221]

Or

 TRUMP: Right, I'm off on holiday. Your president needs a break! Work hard play hard! My mind is never off the ball, but I'll take advantage of 'global warming' and get a bit of sunshine.

Some believe Trump has spent around $99 million on golf trips so far.[222]

220   Twitter, 22 December 2018
221   Twitter, 19 December 2011
222   https://trumpgolfcount.com/

24.

 TRUMP: I like to have fun, I'd be a fun president. I like to make jokes, I like to mock the haters and losers. People shouldn't take themselves so seriously.

Or

 TRUMP: We need a President who isn't a laughing stock to the entire World. We need a truly great leader, a genius at strategy and winning. Respect![223]

I'm just gonna leave that there . . .

25.

 TRUMP: Well, if I ever ran for office, I'd do better as a Democrat than a Republican.[224]

Or

 TRUMP: The Democrats are so self-righteous and ANGRY! Loosen up and have some fun. The Country is doing well![225]

Again, people can change their minds. I'm not sure he would have fared so well as a Democrat. He would have had to delete a LOT of old tweets . . .

26.

 TRUMP: No president ever worked harder than me (cleaning up the mess I inherited)![226]

Or

 TRUMP: I think being president would be too hard. The country is a mess and even though I think I'd be great, the best even, I'd rather be playing golf.

I wonder if the previous presidents agree.

---

223   Twitter, 9 August 2014
224   *Playboy*, March 1990
225   Twitter, 11 February 2019
226   Twitter, 11 February 2019

27

TRUMP: Lets just call them WALLS from now on and stop playing political games! A WALL is a WALL![227]

Or

 FAKE **TRUMP:** It would be a kind of fense. A tall fense. A strong fense. Some would call it a wall. Yes, a wall.

WALL!!

28.

 TRUMP: It's almost like the United States has no President - we are a rudderless ship heading for a major disaster. Good luck everyone![228]

 Or

FAKE **TRUMP:** I'm getting America back on track, steering the ship back home. The great ship. And I'm steering it back to so many happier people

Hopeful words here.

29.

 FAKE **TRUMP:** This job, it's crazy, its hard. It takes a certain type of person to do it well, to do it best. Someone smart and someone who can deal with bigness.

 Or

 TRUMP: Well the one thing I would say – and I say this to people – I never realised how big it was . . . So you know, I really just see the bigness of it all.[229]

America is really big, to be fair.

---

227 Twitter, 31 January 2019
228 Twitter, 19 March 2014
229 Associated Press interview, 2017

30.

 TRUMP: No politician in history – and I say this with great surety – has been treated worse or more unfairly.[230]

Or

 FAKE **TRUMP:** People love me and most people treat me with respect and admiration. They can see what I am doing for the country. Even those that didn't vote for me. They can see what I'm doing for this country and they love me.

Great surety?

31.

 TRUMP: 'We build too many walls and not enough bridges' – Isaac Newton.[231]

Or

FAKE **TRUMP:** 'I am who I am' – Gloria Gaynor.

Yep, Donald Trump tweeted this 'quote' from Isaac Newton. Was he joking? Being ironic? Blasting Isaac for something? Very hard to say.

32.

FAKE **TRUMP:** AMERICA IS STILL NOT RESPECTED! MAGA!

Or

 TRUMP: AMERICA IS RESPECTED AGAIN![232]

He's done his job! Can he go home now?

---

230 Graduation speech to coastguard cadets, 17 May 2017
231 Twitter, 7 October 2013
232 Twitter, 24 December 2018